Dyslexia

below.

The SEN series

Dyslexia

Gavin Reid

continuum
LONDON • NEW YORK

Continuum International Publishing Group

The Tower Building
11 York Road
London
SE1 7NX

15 East 26th Street
New York, NY 10010

www.continuumbooks.com

British Library Cataloguing-in-Publication Data
A catalogue record for this book is available from the British Library.

ISBN: 08264 7579 5 (paperback)

Typeset by Servis Filmsetting Ltd, Manchester
Printed and bound in Great Britain by MPG Books Ltd,
Bodmin, Cornwall

Contents

1

Dyslexia Explained

Background to dyslexia

The term dyslexia is one that many teachers and parents are familiar with, but despite that, many only have a vague understanding of what the term 'dyslexia' actually means. There is still some confusion surrounding dyslexia, and to a certain extent some controversy and uncertainty on the type of teaching intervention that is the most appropriate for children with dyslexia. This book, therefore, aims to provide an explanation of dyslexia so that teachers and parents can be familiar with the term, have a good understanding of dyslexia, know how it is identified and the most effective teaching and learning strategies that can be used in the classroom.

There are a number of key points about dyslexia that teachers need to recognize. These are shown below, and many of these points will be developed and discussed in later chapters:

♦ dyslexia can be seen within a continuum from mild to severe;

♦ the degree, and the impact of dyslexia on the child can vary according to the nature of the task and the nature of the learning context;

Dyslexia

- the difficulties relating to dyslexia are usually associated with literacy, but this may not always be the case;

- the literacy difficulties associated with dyslexia can take the form of difficulty with reading accuracy (decoding), spelling, reading comprehension, reading fluency, reading aloud, expressive writing and copying accurately;

- children with dyslexia can also display other difficulties such as coordination, memory, directional confusion, sequencing, identification of key points and handwriting;

- early identification is important for effective intervention;

- it is widely accepted that dyslexia occurs because the child has difficulty with phonological processing, that is, a difficulty in recognizing and remembering sounds and being able to use those sounds in words;

- there is, however, some evidence that visual and motor difficulties can also be associated with dyslexia. These difficulties may affect visual clarity in reading and coordination and balance;

- dyslexia will not be 'cured', it is a lifelong condition, but the effects of dyslexia can be minimized with effective teaching intervention and adaptations to tasks, through differentiation in the curriculum and accommodations in the workplace;

- the dyslexic person may have many strengths and these strengths may be used to compensate for his/her difficulties.

It can be seen when glancing at these key points that it is important that teachers should have, at least, an awareness of dyslexia as dyslexia can affect many different areas of learning. Additionally, because it occurs within a continuum it is likely that a number of children in the class will be somewhere within that continuum. It is estimated in fact that around 10 to 15 per cent of children may have some degree of dyslexia. A knowledge of dyslexia therefore can assist teachers in planning and developing appropriate tasks and curricular activities for children with dyslexia and this can, to a great extent, minimize the failure in learning that is often experienced by children, even very young children, with dyslexia.

Characteristics of dyslexia

Some of the characteristics of dyslexia were mentioned above in the key points, but the main characteristics are described in more detail below:

Reading

Decoding
This is a difficulty in accurately breaking down words into their constituent parts. For example, the word 'governmental' has to be broken down as follows *gov/ern/men/tal* in order to be decoded. Usually after a reader has seen this word a few times it can be read by sight. Children with dyslexia may have difficulty in breaking words down into their constituent parts and in transferring a word from a decoding strategy to a visual (sight word) strategy. Additionally, children with dyslexia may

3

not have many sight words in their 'known' vocabulary. This means that almost every word, and certainly words that are not commonly used, will need to be decoded, i.e. broken down into their constituent sounds. This can be problematic for the child with dyslexia. In order to do this the reader needs to have some skills in phonemic awareness and be able to recognize the different sounds and groups of letters (syllables) that make up a word. This difficulty with breaking words down into syllables will affect reading fluency. Children with dyslexia may also substitute words when reading aloud, for example saying 'car' for 'bus'.

Fluency
Fluency is important in reading as it aids comprehension. Children with dyslexia usually read by using clues from the context of the passage. In order to do this there has to be some degree of fluency and understanding. Fluency helps to provide understanding and makes it easier for the reader to use context. One way to aid fluency is to use a text that is below the child's reading age, or texts that are characterized by the high interest level and low level vocabulary (Hi-Lo readers). Generally there may be a reluctance to read for pleasure, and any interest at all, in any type of reasonable reading material, should be encouraged.

Comprehension
Reading comprehension can be a problem for the child with dyslexia because of both the difficulties with fluency and the problems in decoding. Yet if the text is read to the child they will very likely understand it as their listening comprehension is usually better than

their reading comprehension. In fact, reading a text to the child, or discussing the text through pre-reading discussion with the child, can each help to develop reading comprehension.

Sequencing
Children with dyslexia often have a sequencing difficulty. This means they may get letters, or parts of a word, in the wrong order. For example, the word *preliminary* may be read as *preinlimary.*

Spelling

The child with dyslexia may show some or all of the following:

♦ difficulty remembering spelling rules;

♦ phonological errors, for example, using the letter 'f' for the sound 'ph';

♦ letters or groups of letters out of sequence;

♦ inconsistent use of some letters with similar sounds such as 's' and 'z';

♦ difficulty with word endings, for example, using 'ie' for 'y';

♦ confusion or omission of vowels.

Writing

Expressive writing
The child with dyslexia will usually show a reluctance to write a lengthy piece of work. Additionally, it may be

difficult for him/her to identify and develop key points. This means that the written piece may be rambling and poorly organized. This underlines the need to provide dyslexic children with a structure when engaging in expressive and creative writing.

Handwriting
Children with dyslexia may have an inconsistent writing style and the slope and characteristics of the writing style can vary within the same sentence. There may be an inconsistent use of capital and small letters. Additionally, the writing speed may be slow, deliberate and hesitant. Sometimes the child may adopt an unusual writing grip or sitting position.

Memory

The child with dyslexia may display indicators of a:

♦ poor short-term memory, which means they will have difficulty remembering lists;

♦ poor long-term memory which could be due to confusion at the time of learning, or poor organizational strategies;

♦ difficulty with recalling information that has been recently learnt but not used a great deal. This is because although they may have learnt the information, it has not been consolidated. The child, therefore, will not have what is known as automaticity in the information that has been learnt. There is some evidence to suggest that children with dyslexia have poor automaticity and can take longer than expected to achieve automaticity in learning. To achieve automaticity the learner needs to use the information in as many different contexts as possible and the information will then be consolidated. In order to do this, children with dyslexia need a significant amount of overlearning.

Children with dyslexia may also show difficulties in the following.

Organization

♦ poor organizational strategies for learning;

♦ poor organization of timetable, materials, equipment and items needed for learning, such as remembering and organizing homework notebook.

Motor development

♦ may have a difficulty with coordination and tasks such as tying shoelaces, hopping and skipping;

♦ may accidentally knock into furniture in the classroom, trip and fall over frequently.

Speech Development

They may show:

♦ confusion over similar sounds in words;

♦ poor articulation;

♦ difficulty blending letters and sounds into words·

♦ poor awareness of rhyme;

♦ poor syntactic structure;

♦ naming difficulties, i.e. remembering the names of objects.

Definitions of dyslexia

Not surprisingly, in view of the range of characteristics associated with dyslexia, different education authorities, and authorities in different countries, may have different definitions of dyslexia. The important point about a definition is that it should be clear and consistent. That means that teachers working in the same education authority should all have the same understanding of dyslexia and there should be consistency in how schools within the authority deal with dyslexia.

Dyslexia organizations such as The British Dyslexia Association (www.bda-dyslexia.org.uk), The International Dyslexia Association (www.interdys.org), The European Dyslexia Association (www.bedford.ac.uk/eda) and the Dyslexia Association of Ireland (www.acld-dyslexia.com) all have definitions of dyslexia, and they are all different. Certainly there are some commonalities within the different definitions; such as dyslexia being life long, it can be seen within a continuum and that one of the main features of dysle̶ ̶ ̶ ̶ncerns literacy development. A compre-
̶ ̶ ̶ ̶ ̶ition of dyslexia has been developed by
̶ ̶ ̶ is shown below.

̶cessing difference experienced by people
characterised by difficulties in literacy, it

8

can affect other cognitive areas such as memory, speed of processing, time management, co-ordination and directional aspects. There may be visual and phonological difficulties and there is usually some discrepancy in performances in different areas of learning. It is important that the individual differences and learning styles are acknowledged since these will affect outcomes of learning and assessment. It is also important to consider the learning and work context as the nature of the difficulties associated with dyslexia may well be more pronounced in some learning situations. (Reid 2003, pp. 4–5)

There are some key factors regarding this definition. The important phrases in the definition above are:

♦ *processing difference*

♦ *experienced by people of all ages*

♦ *difficulties in literacy*

♦ *it can affect other cognitive areas*

♦ *discrepancy in performances*

♦ *important to consider the learning and work context*

It can be noted from the information above that there can be wide-ranging difficulties associated with dyslexia. It is unlikely the child with dyslexia will show all of these, but some of these will certainly be evident. An important consideration in relation to these characteristics noted above is how these factors will affect children with dyslexia, their self-esteem, their motivation, and indeed skills, in learning.

How dyslexia affects children's learning

One of the key factors about learning is that learning is a process. This process can be described as a dynamic one. This means that different parts of the brain interact with other parts and each relies on and interacts with the other. For example, the various parts of the brain that deal with visual/auditory/memory/understanding/coordination may all be used simultaneously to tackle a task. It is often this simultaneous use of learning skills that is challenging for children with dyslexia. For that reason tasks need to be structured, simplified and preferably focused towards the child's stronger areas of learning. Children with dyslexia are usually stronger visually or kinesthetically, as opposed to auditory. That means initial learning will be more meaningful if presented visually or through the experience of learning (kinesthetic).

Kinesthetic experiences can be helpful to reinforce learning. Kinesthetic means experiencing learning. So activities that involve drama and role-playing, or investigation and enquiry activities, such as in a survey, interview or questionnaire, all utilize kinesthetic skills because each of these activities involves experiential learning.

Information processing

One of the key considerations in relation to how children with dyslexia learn is how effective they are at utilizing their learning skills when learning a piece of information. Whether it is learning to read a word, or learning a spelling rule or understanding some aspect of History, Geography or Science all learners engage in a learning process. This process is essentially a cycle of learning activities called the information processing cycle (see the box below).

The Information Processing Cycle

♦ **Input** – auditory, visual, tactile, kinesthetic

♦ **Cognition** – memory, understanding, organizing and making sense of information

♦ **Output** – reading aloud, talking, discussing, drawing, seeing, experiencing

---

Cognition

Cognition is important for learning. This describes the actual processes involved in learning a piece of information. This relates to memory, understanding, organizing and generally making sense of information. Often children with dyslexia have what can be described as cognitive difficulties. This includes memory and organizing information, and often these are quite serious difficulties that the dyslexic child needs to overcome for effective learning.

What is important however, is that good teaching can help to overcome all of these cognitive difficulties. Much can be done to aid the child's memory, and assistance by the teacher to help the dyslexic child organize information can help him/her learn more effectively. The teacher can play a key role, therefore, in helping dyslexic children overcome cognitive difficulties.

Metacognition

Cognition, as indicated above, means learning; metacognition means learning to learn. This implies that children can be taught to be more effective learners. This is very important for dyslexic children. The research indicates that children with dyslexia may be weak in metacognitive awareness and therefore have difficulty in knowing how to go about tackling a problem. This means they may not be sure on *how* to, for example, interpret a question or to work out the most efficient way of answering it; or in fact to remember any piece of information. The development of metacognitive skills can be aided by programmes that are essentially 'study skills' programmes. Often study skills are seen to be part of examination preparation, but in fact this is too late. Study skills, particularly for learners with dyslexia, should be provided as young as possible. Becoming efficient in studying and learning helps the learner make connections between different pieces of information and this can help with transfer of learning and generally more efficient use of information. This will be discussed further in Chapter 3.

Self-esteem

Self-esteem is important for learning. A child will learn more effectively and will be more motivated to learn if his/her self-esteem is high. This is also very important for learners with dyslexia. Young children with dyslexia, very soon after commencing formal education, quickly realize that some aspects of school education, such as reading, spelling and writing are challenging for them.

This can result in feelings of failure and frustration. This can lower the child's motivation and self-esteem in relation to learning. Effort needs to be made to ensure children with dyslexia are provided with opportunities to gain some success, as it is only through success that self-esteem will be enhanced. Activities such as Circle Time (Mosley 1996) can help to provide opportunities for enhancement of self-esteem.

How the teacher and the school can help

Many of the points mentioned above will benefit all learners. This is important as it indicates that good and effective teaching practices will greatly aid children with dyslexia without the necessity of having to resort to expensive, commercially produced programmes. It is certainly important to know about these pro-grammes and these will be discussed later in this book. It is also important to appreciate the characteristics of dyslexia and to recognize that children with dyslexia need to be seen as individuals, as each child may show different characteristics to varying degrees.

Communication between the school and home

One of the important aspects in dealing with dyslexia is communication. Often the controversy and confu-sion that can exist in the field of dyslexia results from a breakdown in effective communication between the school and the home. There are many conflicting views on how dyslexia can be dealt with. Some of these con-flicting views emerge from information in commercial websites and other types of uncontrolled and often untested commercial outlets. It is important that the school should be able to advise on the suitability of programmes for dyslexic children. This can be done by assuring parents that the best is being done for their child, which can be achieved by the school communicating with parents effectively. This means informing parents how the school has recognized the dyslexic characteristics of the child and how they are meeting his/her needs. It is important to reassure parents that the school does take dyslexia seriously, otherwise parents will be swayed by persuasively appealing commercially orientated programmes that purport to claim unrivalled successes. It is useful if the school has a member of staff who has undertaken training in dyslexia, and this person can provide information to parents on any new programme that they may have seen advertised on the internet or elsewhere.

Communication within the school

It is crucial that there is good communication within the school. This is particularly important in larger primary and in most secondary schools. Good communication will allow essential information to be passed between teachers. Although each dyslexic child needs to be seen as an individual, many of the strategies utilize similar principles, and teachers can share experiences with colleagues. Dyslexia is therefore a whole-school concern and teachers should not feel that it is their problem alone. Schools can quite quickly build up a bank of resources and strategies for dyslexic children.

Summary of Chapter 1

The key points in this chapter are:

♦ dyslexia is a term that can easily be misunderstood;

♦ dyslexia can be seen in a continuum from mild to severe;

♦ children with dyslexia can show different characteristics and therefore their needs should be addressed on an individual basis;

♦ although the principal difficulties associated with dyslexia relate to literacy – reading, writing and spelling – children with dyslexia can also show other difficulties relating to memory, coordination and organization;

♦ it is important to identify and recognize the strengths shown by children with dyslexia, and to attempt to incorporate these strengths into a teaching programme;

♦ knowing how children learn and how to make learning more effective through study skills and good teaching practices can be extremely beneficial for children with dyslexia;

♦ there is a wide range of commercially produced reading programmes that can augment teaching intervention with children with dyslexia;

♦ it is important to consider the role of the curriculum and the processes involving differentiation and learning styles as these can help children with dyslexia understand the task more clearly and undertake learning more effectively;

Dyslexia

♦ finally, it is important to recognize the need to boost the self-esteem of children with dyslexia as it is too easy for them to become discouraged and lose interest in learning.

2

Spotting Dyslexia

Key issues and questions

There are a number of key issues and questions related to identifying dyslexia. These include:

♦ Who is responsible for identifying dyslexia?

♦ What is the difference between screening and formal assessment?

♦ At what age can dyslexia be reliably identified?

♦ How reliable are short screening tests?

♦ What is the role of the class teacher in assessment?

♦ What is the role of professionals and parents in assessment?

♦ What kinds of assessments are there?

♦ How can we be sure it is dyslexia?

There is no simple answer to these questions, particularly since criteria for identifying dyslexia can vary from country to country and within countries. There are, however, some general points that can provide guidance in answering these questions.

Who is responsible for identifying dyslexia?

This can vary but the class teacher is well placed to initially spot if the child is displaying early signs or characteristics of dyslexia. It is for this reason that the class teacher should have some training and an understanding of dyslexia, and early years teachers in particular should be able to identify the characteristics that can be associated with dyslexia.

An initial suspicion of dyslexia can be followed up with a more formal short screening test. Such a test can be given by the class teacher as they usually do not need any training to administer. Class teachers, however, may need to consult with other professionals, perhaps a learning support teacher or a teacher with responsibility for special needs, in order to gain maximum benefit from interpreting the results of a screening test.

There are a number of more formal and standardized instruments that can be used to identify dyslexia. Some of these are discussed later in this chapter. An educational psychologist is usually involved in the formal identification process because they can access certain tests, such as IQ tests, that are categorized as 'closed tests' (meaning only certain professionals with suitable training can use them).

What is the difference between screening and formal assessment?

A screening test is usually a short general test or questionnaire. Some screening tests however, such as the *Dyslexia Screening Tests* (Fawcett and Nicolson 1996), the *Listening and Literacy Index* (Weedon and Reid 2001), and computer-assisted tests such as the *Cognitive Profiling System* (Singleton 1996) can be quite sophisticated and well standardized. Usually a screening provides an indication that dyslexia may be present.

A more formal assessment can involve input from a number of professionals, such as educational psychologists, speech and language therapists, occupational therapists and specialist teachers. Formal assessment will usually include a range of tests on reading, spelling and number work as well as tests on memory skills, coordination, dominance and cognitive abilities. The process of a formal assessment may extend over a period of time and there would need to be some input from parents.

At what age can dyslexia be reliably identified?

This can be a controversial issue. There are a number of screening tests for dyslexia that can be administered to children as young as three. Generally speaking, however, during the pre-school stage characteristics can be identified, without actually providing a definitive diagnosis of dyslexia. Children who display dyslexic characteristics can be described as 'high risk' – children who may have dyslexia or will have significant difficulties in literacy acquisition. It is important to identify 'high risk' children so they can be closely monitored.

Usually children are around six to seven before they can be reliably identified as dyslexic, and it may be later in some children. It is not unusual, in fact, for young people to be first identified as dyslexic at high school or when entering college and university. But increasingly there is a move towards early identification because the intervention becomes more successful. If children are not identified until later in their education this is usually because they have not been formally assessed, or because they have compensated quite successfully for their dyslexic difficulties by using their strengths. Many children and adults are able to compensate quite successfully.

How reliable are short screening tests?

Short screening tests provide information on the child very quickly. Whether the responses to these questions or tasks amount to a diagnosis of dyslexia is quite another matter. Screening tests provide information and will be useful as they inform on the child's learning behaviours. In order, however, to convert this information into a diagnosis of dyslexia, further detailed assessments will need to be conducted. For instance, information on the child's learning pattern and learning behaviours, and his/her performances with class work will also be required.

What is the role of the class teacher in assessment?

There are a number of potential dyslexic characteristics the class teacher can observe at various stages within the classroom. These are detailed below.

Pre-school and early years

Concern may be raised if the child shows some or all of the following:

♦ forgetfulness

♦ speech difficulty

♦ reversal of letters

♦ difficulty remembering letters of the alphabet

♦ difficulty remembering the sequence of letters of the alphabet

♦ if there is a history of dyslexia in the family

♦ coordination difficulties, e.g. bumping into tables and chairs

♦ difficulty with tasks which require fine motor skills, such as tying shoelaces

♦ slow at reacting to some tasks

♦ reluctance to concentrate on a task for a reasonable period of time

♦ confusing words which sound similar

♦ reluctance to go to school

♦ signs of not enjoying school

♦ reluctance to read

♦ difficulty learning words and letters

♦ difficulty with phonics (sounds)

♦ poor memory

21

- losing items
- difficulty forming and writing letters
- difficulty copying
- difficulty colouring
- poor organization of materials.

Primary School

After around two years at school:

- hesitant at reading and therefore has poor reading fluency
- poor word skills – difficulty decoding new words and breaking these words down into syllables
- poor knowledge of the sounds of words
- difficulty recognizing where in words particular sounds come
- spelling difficulties
- substitution of words when reading, for example 'bus' for 'car'.

Later stages in primary school:

- as above, and also behaviour difficulties
- frustration
- may show abilities in other areas of the curriculum apart from reading
- attention and concentration difficulties.

Secondary

♦ as above, and also, takes a long time over home-work

♦ misreads words

♦ relies on others to tell him/her information

♦ poor general knowledge

♦ takes longer than others on written tasks

♦ may not write a lot in comparison to his/her knowledge of the subject

♦ difficulty copying from books

♦ may spend a great deal of time studying with little obvious benefit

♦ may not finish class work or examinations because he/she runs out of time

♦ there may be a degree of unhappiness because of difficulties in school that will manifest itself in other areas.

It is important that professionals within the school liaise in identification and assessment as the difficulties may take on a different form in different stages of education. Communication is vitally important in both the identification and the support of the child, and communication between home and school is also extremely vital. Assessment should not be the responsibility of one individual teacher or psychologist, but an interactive process between parents, teachers and psychologists. This interactive process should make it possible to ascertain if the child has dyslexic difficulties, and any diagnosis will utilize information from a number of people.

What is the role of the professionals in assessment?

Below are some suggestions of the role for each of those involved in the assessment process.

Class teachers can note:

♦ the child's reading and spelling pattern

♦ unexpected lack of progress in either reading or spelling

♦ difficulty with rhyming and sounds

♦ poor memory

♦ inconsistency in performances.

Learning support/specialist teachers can access the above information but may also use:

♦ standardized tests such as the Phonological Assessment Battery, Phonological Abilities Test, Dyslexia Screening Test, Listening and Literacy Index

♦ discrepancy criteria relating to the discrepancy between decoding and listening comprehension

♦ extended observation and interview with the child

♦ diagnostic analysis of spelling errors, such as miscue analysis.

Psychologists can undertake an assessment or comment on the results of the above, but also can access 'closed' tests such as:

◆ Wechsler Intelligence Scale for Children
◆ British Abilities Test
◆ other cognitive and intelligence tests.

Parents can provide information on:

◆ how their son/daughter copes with learning at home
◆ social skills and emotional maturity
◆ memory/coordination
◆ any area of confusion and anxiety.

Diagnosis relies on obtaining a variety of information from a range of sources, and it is important that all available sources of information are called on as far as possible. While the label 'dyslexia' is useful, it should not be essential in order to access appropriate support. In practice, however, in some countries and education authorities, a label seems to be almost a prerequisite for specific and specialized support. This includes support in examinations.

Nevertheless, since dyslexia is a continuum, the label should not be too readily applied, particularly if the profile indicates a borderline type of profile and is not clear cut. This, however, should not prevent appropriate support and teaching as the information from the assessment should help to inform possible avenues for teaching, and identify programmes that may be helpful.

All assessment data, whether it leads to a diagnosis or not, should inform teaching, this is a crucial point in an assessment. Assessment should help to provide explanations for any concern over lack of progress, and importantly, provide pointers for appropriate resources and teaching. Assessment and a diagnosis is therefore the beginning, not the end of the process. All roads need to lead to effective and appropriate intervention.

Different types of assessment

Teacher assessment

Much of the teacher assessment can be carried out within the normal assessment procedures in the classroom. Teachers have a responsibility to monitor children's progress and record keeping and ongoing assessment is now very much part of a teacher's role. Lack of progress based on the results of formal tests, or lack of expected progress based on the child's classroom performances can alert the teacher that a child may have some significant difficulty.

Quite apart from formal tests, the teacher can obtain a lot of information from observation. A framework for observation is shown later in this chapter.

Phonological assessment

There is a great deal of research that supports the 'phonological representation hypothesis' as a key factor in explaining the difficulties experienced by children with dyslexia. It means the principal difficulty in dyslexia relates to phonological development, and it is important that some form of phonological assessment is carried out. There are a number of commercially available phonological tests, as well as other phonological tests that are integrated into teaching programmes. But it is also possible for teachers to develop their own phonological assessment.

Adams (1990) reviewed various phonological tasks and was able to identify at least five levels of difficulty:

♦ knowledge of nursery rhymes which involves only an ear for the sounds of words;

♦ awareness of rhyme and alliteration which requires both sensitivity to the sounds and an ability to focus on certain sounds;

♦ blending of phonemes and splitting of syllables to identify phonemes – this demands an awareness that words can be subdivided into smaller sounds;

♦ phoneme segmentation requires a thorough understanding that words can be analysed into a series of phonemes;

♦ phoneme manipulation requires a child not only to understand and produce phonemes, but also to be able to manipulate them by addition, deletion or transposition.

It is important that assessment of phonological ability should identify the specific aspects of the different types of phonological tasks that can contribute to the reading process.

Hatcher and Snowling (2002) suggest that the following can be used:

- rhyme recognition and detection tests;
- rhyme oddity tasks that present the child with a set of three or four spoken words and requires the child to identify which is the one that does not belong to a group;
- alliteration tasks that assess the ability to isolate initial sounds in words are all phonological awareness tasks;
- naming speed;
- fluency tests are useful as these assess the speed of phonological production.

The phonological skills that children need for reading include:

- rhyme production;
- syllable blending;
- phoneme blending;
- phoneme segmentation.

According to Gorrie and Parkinson (1995), a phonological assessment should cover the following areas:

- polysyllabic word/non-word repetition and recognition;
- syllable segmentation, deletion of prefixes and suffixes, and deletion of syllables;
- intra-syllable segmentation, such as detection of onset and rime;

♦ phoneme segmentation such as blending, detection and deletion of initial and final phonemes.

Some phonological assessments can be very sophisticated and specialist. Most, however, can be readily administered by the class teacher and can provide a detailed and ongoing record of the child's development in the sub-skills needed for reading.

As indicated above, the class teacher can obtain a lot of information from observation. When embarking on any type of classroom observation it is useful to develop a framework first in order to guide and record the observations. An example of such a framework is shown on page 31.

Curriculum assessment

Formal assessment can provide some information but it is also necessary to note how the child performs with tasks presented as part of the class curriculum. It is important to note how the child tackles specific tasks, the type of tasks that prove difficult, and how aspects of the task can be adapted to enable the learner to succeed. This form of assessment can be very instrumental in the development of individual educational programmes. It can inform on the areas of priority and the setting of targets for an Individual Educational Plan.

Miscue analysis during oral reading

The system known as miscue analysis can offer a structure to investigate reading errors in a natural manner using curriculum-related text. Miscue analysis assumes that miscues occur systematically and occur whether reading is silent or aloud and that the degree of sense the child makes of the material reflects his/her use of prior knowledge. The marking system that is usually adopted in miscue analysis is indicated below:

Omissions
These may occur in relation to reading speed – for example, when the child's normal silent reading speed is used when reading orally. As the child progresses in reading ability and reading speed increases, omissions may still be noted as they tend to increase as the reading speed does.

Additions
These may reflect superficial reading with perhaps an over-dependence on context clues.

Substitutions
These can be visual or semantic substitutions. In younger readers, substitutions would tend to be visual and in older readers contextual. In the latter case they may reflect an over-dependence on context clues.

Repetitions
These may indicate poor directional attack, and perhaps some anticipatory uncertainty on the part of the reader about a word to be read.

Reversals
These may reflect the lack of left-right orientation. Reversals may also indicate some visual difficulty and perhaps a lack of reading for meaning.

Hesitations
These can occur when the reader is unsure of the text and perhaps lacking in confidence in reading. For the same reason that repetitions may occur, the reader may also be anticipating a different word later in the sentence.

Self-corrections
These would occur when the reader becomes more aware of meaning and less dependent on simple word recognition.

Framework for observation

Attention

♦ Length of attention span?

♦ Conditions when attention is enhanced?

♦ Factors contributing to any distractibility?

♦ Attention/distractibility under different learning conditions?

Organization

♦ Organizational preferences?

♦ Degree of structure required?

♦ Organization of work, desk, self?

♦ Reactions to imposed organization?

Sequencing

♦ Able to follow sequence with aid?

♦ General difficulty with sequencing: work; carrying out instructions; words when reading; individual letters in written work?

Interaction

♦ Degree of interaction with peers and adults?

♦ Preferred interaction – one-to-one, small groups or whole class?

♦ How is interaction sustained?

Language

♦ Expressive language?

♦ Is meaning accurately conveyed?

♦ Spontaneous/prompted?

♦ Is there appropriate use of natural breaks in speech?

♦ Expressive language in different contexts, e.g. one-to-one, small group, class group?

♦ Errors, omissions and difficulties in conversation and responses, e.g. mispronunciations, questions to be repeated or clarified?

Comprehension

♦ How does the child comprehend information?

♦ What type of cues most readily facilitate comprehension?

♦ Use of schema?

♦ What type of instructions are most easily understood – written, oral or visual?

♦ How readily can knowledge be transferred to other areas?

Reading

♦ Reading preferences – aloud, silent?

♦ Type of errors?

Visual

♦ Discrimination between letters which look the same?

♦ Inability to appreciate that the same letter may look different, e.g. 'G' 'g'?

♦ Omitting or transposing part of a word (this could indicate a visual segmentation difficulty)?

Auditory

♦ Difficulties in auditory discrimination?

♦ Inability to hear consonant sounds in initial, medial or final position?

♦ Auditory sequencing?

♦ Auditory blending?

♦ Auditory segmentation?

Motivation/initiative

♦ Interest level of child?

♦ How is motivation increased, what kind of prompting and cueing is necessary?

♦ To what extent does the child take responsibility for own learning?

♦ What kind of help is required?

Self-concept

♦ What tasks are more likely to be tackled with confidence?

♦ When is confidence low?

♦ Self-concept and confidence in different contexts?

Relaxation

♦ Is the child relaxed when learning?

♦ Evidence of tension and relaxation?

Learning preferences

These include the following learning preferences:

♦ Auditory?

♦ Visual?

♦ Oral?

♦ Kinesthetic?

♦ Tactile?

♦ Global?

♦ Analytic?

The above can provide an overview of how the child performs in the learning situation. This is important for dyslexia as the performance of dyslexic children can vary in different situations and with different aspects of the curriculum. It is crucial, therefore, to observe the child in different learning situations.

How can we be sure it is dyslexia?

Perhaps one of the frequently asked questions regarding identification of dyslexia is how can one be sure the child has dyslexia and not some other, or indeed a combination of, difficulties. There are many issues inherent in this question and it underlines the view that to identify dyslexia the teacher and the school need to embark on a process which should consider other factors apart from test results. The curriculum, learning style, the child's history, performances in different situations and with different tasks and the views and information that can be gleaned from parents are all important. The situation is made more complex by the lack of clear criteria that can distinguish dyslexia in a child who has other specific learning difficulties such as dyspraxia, attention disorders, specific language impairment and many others. In a number of children dyslexia can overlap with other specific learning difficulties and it can be quite challenging to disentangle the different characteristics that contribute to each of the specific learning difficulties. Weedon and Reid (2003) have attempted to do this through the development of a screening process called *SNAP* (*Special Needs Assessment Profile*) (see also www.hoddertests.co.uk and www.SNAPassessment.com).

The *Special Needs Assessment Profile* is a computer-aided diagnostic assessment and profiling package that makes it possible to 'map' each student's own mix of difficulties on to an overall matrix of learning, behavioural and other difficulties. From this, clusters and patterns of weaknesses and strengths help to identify the core features of a student's difficulties – visual, dyslexic, dyspraxic, phonological, attention, or any other of the 15 key deficits targeted – and suggests a diagnosis that points the way forward for that individual student. It provides a structured profile that yields an overview at the early stages of 'School Action' in the Code of Practice – and also informs the process of external referral at 'School Action Plus'.

SNAP involves four steps:

Step 1 *(Pupil Assessment Pack)*: structured questionnaire checklists for completion by class teachers and parents give an initial 'outline map' of the child's difficulties.

Step 2 *(CD-ROM)*: the SENCO or Learning Support staff charts the child's difficulties, using the CD-ROM to identify patterns and target any further diagnostic follow-up assessments to be carried out at Step 3.

Step 3 *(User's Kit)*: focused assessments from a photocopiable resource bank of quick diagnostic 'probes' yield a detailed and textured understanding of the child's difficulties.

Step 4 *(CD-ROM)*: the computer-generated profile yields specific guidance on support (including person-alized information sheets for parents) and practical follow-up.

SNAP helps to facilitate the collaboration between different groups of professionals, and between profes-sionals and parents. This is extremely vital in order to obtain a full picture of the student's abilities and diffi-culties. There is a dedicated website that contains a number of ideas on the teaching issues associated with 15 different specific learning difficulties. The website is www.SNAPassessment.com. This type of tool can be particularly useful in identifying and decid-ing on teaching priorities for children with dyslexia and other specific learning difficulties.

Discrepancies

One of the ways of distinguishing between dyslexia and perhaps a child who is not reading because he/she has a general learning difficulty is to focus on the discrepancies in his/her classroom performances. A dyslexic child will very likely be able to communi-cate and embark on oral discussion to a higher level than would be anticipated on the basis of his/her written work. A discrepancy between written and oral work is often characteristic of dyslexia. Additionally the discrepancy between listening com-prehension and reading accuracy (decoding) can also be noted. These factors can often distinguish a child with dyslexia from one that has difficulty in learning across a number of cognitive areas. Children who have difficulties across a number of areas are also likely to have difficulties in comprehension, including listening comprehension.

Summary of Chapter 2

This chapter has

♦ identified some of the key issues in relation to identification of dyslexia;

♦ indicated that identification and assessment is a process and should involve a number of school professionals and parents;

♦ provided some insights into some of the tests and strategies that can be used for dyslexia, indicating that screening tests can readily be used by teachers but these will only provide a guide and pinpoint 'at risk' factors;

♦ highlighted the role of phonological assessment in identifying dyslexia;

♦ provided some guidance for the class teacher in relation to observation and how this can provide useful information in the identification of dyslexia;

♦ indicated that it is important to consider curriculum assessment and to analyse how the child performs with different types of tasks;

♦ provided guidance on the need to distinguish between dyslexia and other specific learning difficulties such as dyspraxia and specific language impairment;

♦ indicated that children with dyslexia can often display a number of discrepancies in different areas of the curriculum and this can help to identify educational priorities for the child.

3

Teaching Approaches

There is a considerable range of programmes available that can be suitable for children with dyslexia. Some of these programmes are highly specialized and aimed at teachers with a detailed knowledge of dyslexia. Many programmes, however, can be readily accessed by the class teacher without much experience of dyslexia. Moreover, it can be suggested that intervention for children with dyslexia is as much about **good teaching** as accessing specialized programmes. Most of the teaching approaches for dyslexia are based on a number of principles and these principles can be adapted into everyday teaching procedures.

Some principles for teaching children with dyslexia

Multisensory

All teaching programmes and procedures for children with dyslexia should be multisensory. This means they should incorporate elements of all the modalities – visual, auditory, kinesthetic and tactile. This is important because quite often children with dyslexia have weaknesses in the auditory modality and they need to utilize the other modalities to compensate for these weaknesses.

Sequential

Teaching needs to follow a sequence and this should be structured into small steps so that a progression can be noted. The children should also be able to note this progress.

Overlearning

Children with dyslexia constantly require the learning of new skills to be reinforced. Overlearning is the most appropriate way to do this. This should not take the form of rote repetition, but rather should be carried out by using a range of materials and tasks to highlight the new material or skill that is learnt. In this way teaching will be reinforcing. This will help the new skill to be transferred from short-term memory to long-term memory, thereby retaining the skill for future use.

Materials and activities that can develop overlearning:

♦ picture cards beginning or ending with specific sounds;

♦ games where children have to think of the most words ending in that particular letter sound;

♦ recognition of key words;

♦ vowel discrimination games that help to increase auditory awareness and improve word attack skills;

♦ memory games;

- sequencing activities;

- mnemonics;

- free writing games;

- rhyme songs.

Metacognitive

This means that the child should be able to transfer the new information to other learning. There is some research to indicate that dyslexic children make poor use of metacognitive strategies. This means that learning is not very efficient and they may take a long time to learn new material because they are not able to effectively access previous knowledge. It is important to help the child bridge new information with previously learnt information. Metacognition means thinking about thinking and how the learner questions him/herself on how a particular response was arrived at. This self-questioning can help the learner develop strategies for future learning.

Programmes and approaches

Teaching programmes for dyslexic children should include the following:

- phonological aspects;

- attention and listening;

- the development of spoken language;

- development of fine motor skills;

♦ handwriting;

♦ sequencing;

♦ directionality;

♦ development of short- and long-term memory skills.

Additionally, a programme needs to fit into the overall context of the classroom environment. The role of the school ethos and the holistic nature of the intervention required for children with dyslexia cannot be underestimated.

Some specific programmes and approaches are described below:

Toe by Toe, Multisensory Manual for Teachers and Parents

Toe by Toe (Cowling and Cowling 1998) is a multisensory teaching method highly recommended for teachers and parents. The programme has a multisensory element, a phonic element with some focus on the student's memory through the planning and the timing of each of the lessons in the book. It can be readily used by parents and the instructions are very clear. The same author also has published a programme called Stride Ahead – An Aid to Comprehension (Cowling 2001) which can be a useful follow up to Toe by Toe. Essentially, Stride Ahead has been written for children who can read but may have difficulty in understanding what they are reading.

Interactive literacy games

Crossbow Education and other companies specialize in games for children with dyslexia and produce activities on literacy, numeracy and study skills. These include 'Spingoes', an onset and rime spinner bingo game which comprises a total of 120 games using onset and rime and 'FUNICS' a practical handbook of activities to help children recognize and use rhyming words, blend and segment syllables, identify initial phonemes and link sounds to symbols. 'FUNICS' is produced by Maggie Ford and Anne Tottman and available from Crossbow Education (see page 109). Crossbow also produce literacy games including 'Alphabet Lotto', which focuses on early phonics; 'Bing-Bang-Bong' and 'CVC Spring', which help develop competence in short vowel sounds; and 'Deebees' which is a stick and circle board game to deal with b/d confusion. They also have a board games called 'Magic-E', 'Spinit 'and 'Hotwords' – a five-board set for teaching and reinforcing 'h' sounds such as 'wh', 'sh', 'ch', 'th', 'ph','gh' and silent 'h'; 'Oh No' is a times table photocopiable game book; and 'Tens 'n' Units', which consists of spinning board games which help children of all ages practise the basics of place value in addition and subtraction.

Multi-Sensory Learning

Multi-Sensory Learning produce games which include homophone games designed to improve spelling and recognition of 120 key words. The pack includes lotto scorers and coloured counters; a vowel discrimination game which helps to increase auditory awareness and improve word attack skills; domino word chunks and a dyslexia games manual which has 50 pages of games and activities suitable for all ages in photocopiable format. The manual includes word games, memory games, sequencing activities, mnemonics, free writing suggestions and rhyme songs.

Language experience

It is also important that top-down approaches to reading are considered, so dyslexic children can receive an enriched language experience. This can be achieved through discussion and activities such as paired reading. It is important that even if the child cannot access the print content of some books, the language, concepts and narratives should be discussed. This helps to make literacy motivating, and emphasizes the view that literacy is more than just reading. Literacy embraces many of the social conventions in society and is a powerful tool for social awareness, essential for young people when they leave school. Literacy also has a powerful cognitive component and can help to develop thinking skills in young children as long as reading is seen as much more than accuracy. That is one of the reasons why the experience of extended language and language concepts are important even though the child may not have that level of reading accuracy.

Thrass (The Teaching of Handwriting, Reading and Spelling)

'The Teaching of Handwriting, Reading and Spelling Programme' known as THRASS can be useful as a support approach and as an individualized programme. THRASS has many different aspects that can be accessed by children and parents. Details of these can be found in the comprehensive THRASS web page: www.thrass.com.

Reading fluency

The Hi-Lo readers from LDA, Cambridge and other similar books, such as those from Barrington Stoke Ltd, can be beneficial in relation to motivation. These books have been written with the reluctant reader in mind and they can help children with dyslexia with reading fluency and also help to develop reading comprehension and reading speed.

Multisensory Teaching System for Reading (MTSR)

This is a well-evaluated programme. The programe was designed to promote phonological awareness, ensure overlearning and to give time for review and attainment mastery. It is based on cumulative, structured sequential multisensory delivery with frequent small steps. The authors (Johnson, Philips and Peer 1999) conducted a research study into the use of the programme and found, as well as the above, it also encourages independent learning and improves self-esteem.

Phonological awareness approaches

There is strong evidence to suggest that phonological factors are of considerable importance in reading.

Children with decoding problems appear to be considerably hampered in reading because they are unable to generalize from one word to another. This means that every word they read is unique, indicating that there is a difficulty in learning and applying phonological rules in reading. It therefore emphasizes the importance of teaching sounds/phonemes and ensuring that the child has an awareness of the sound/letter correspondence. Learning words by sight can enable some children to reach a certain standard in reading, but prevents them from adequately tackling new words and extending their vocabulary.

If children have a difficulty with phonological awareness they are more likely to guess the word from the first letter cue and not the first **sound**. This means that the word 'kite' will be tackled from the starting point of the letter 'k' and not the sound 'ki', so the dyslexic reader may well read something like 'kept'. It is important, therefore, that beginning readers receive some structured training in the grapheme/phoneme correspondence. This is particularly necessary for dyslexic children who would not automatically, or readily, appreciate the importance of phonic rules in reading.

Phonic Code Cracker

Phonic Code Cracker (Russell, 1993 revised 2000) is a set of materials subdivided into twelve units, each unit covering a different aspect of teaching literacy, e.g. Unit 3 deals with initial and final consonant blends, Unit 5 deals with common word endings and Unit 9 deals with common silent letters.

Phonic Code Cracker is a very comprehensive and teacher-friendly set of materials. It provides intensive phonic practice for children who have been having difficulty acquiring basic literacy skills. It has been successfully used with children with specific reading difficulties in mainstream primary and secondary schools. Essentially, the scheme consists of support materials and can be successfully used in combination with other schemes. Precision teaching methods are used, but no timescale is recommended as the author acknowledges that each child will have a different rate of learning. Assessment of the pupil's progress is measured through the use of pupil record skills. There are also fluency tests, time targets, accompanying computer software and – very important for building self-esteem – a mastery certificate which the child can retain as a record of his/her achievement.

'Start to Finish' books

The series of 'Start to Finish' books (Don Johnston, www.donjohnston.com) can be beneficial as the series is designed to boost reading and comprehension skills and provides a reader profile, a computer book, audiocassette and paperback book. Designed to engage children in reading real literature, the series can help with fluency and motivation. Some of the topics included in the series are history, famous people, sports, original mysteries and retellings of classic literature. Johnston also produces some excellent software for children with literacy difficulties. This includes 'Write:OutLoud3'. This programme supports each step of the writing process including:

♦ generating ideas – helps with brainstorming and researching topics;

♦ expressing ideas – this allows children to hear their words as they write;

♦ editing work – using a spellchecker designed to check for phonetic misspellings;

♦ revising for meaning – helps with word finding and improves written expression.

Differentiated texts

An example of this is the series of differentiated texts by Hodder Wayland. They produce a series of books with two books on each of the themes covered. These texts cover diverse topics such as World War 2, floods, the world's continents, energy, and cultural festivals. The differentiated text differs in that it has a reduced text length, a more open page layout, bullet points to help with accessing information, clear type face, captions in different print from the main text and the glossary and index use more simplified vocabulary from the text which is not differentiated.

Information and Communication Technology (ICT)

Teachers need to have, or be able to access,

♦ a range of knowledge sources about technology and have some

♦ knowledge of the hardware and software that is available to support the dyslexic child's individual needs.

Technology can be extremely useful for children with dyslexia. Computers can therefore be dyslexic-friendly. Technology can be useful in the following ways.

Reading

Talking books can be very useful for dyslexic children. They provide simultaneous visual and auditory responses ensuring that the text is both seen and heard by the child. In the UK two popular reading schemes have talking books available – 'Wellington Square' (Granada) and 'Oxford Reading Tree' (Sherston). These can be very useful for children with dyslexia as they can help develop independence in reading and obtain meaning more readily as they will not have to concentrate to the same extent on decoding.

Many talking books have additional onscreen activities to support literacy skills, such as phonics, spelling and comprehension and can also be available in non-fiction texts. Examples of these are 'Find Out & Write About' (Crick) and 'Spin Out Stories' (REM).

Creative writing

Creative writing can be challenging for children with dyslexia because it utilizes many different skills simultaneously. ICT can help minimize some of these difficulties and support the child in a number of ways:

♦ onscreen wordbanks – these are dedicated onscreen wordbanks ('Clicker 4' (Crick)) that allow both speech and pictorial support on screen;

♦ the use of a digital camera to support writing. This can help with sequencing, memory, prompts and developing a narrative;

♦ predictive programs with speech, to use with a wordprocessor where typed text is required. Children are offered a choice of words onscreen to enter into their text. This can help to generate an appropriate vocabulary and aid spelling;

♦ wordprocessing as a tool removes the laborious task of copying out written drafts and it also enhances presentation;

♦ a visual concept map approach that will convert to linear text such as the programme called 'Kidspiration/ Inspiration' (REM);

♦ 'draft builders' that offer a more linear approach and help to develop drafts;

♦ portable writing aids such as 'Dreamwriter 500' (Dreamwriter Solutions Ltd) and 'Alphasmart 3000' (iansyst);

♦ handheld spellcheckers, particularly those models that interpret phonic attempts and can encourage self-correction.

'Text Help'

The computer programme known as 'TextHelp' is particularly useful for assisting with essay writing. 'TextHelp' has a read back facility and has a spellchecker that includes a dyslexic spellcheck option that searches for common dyslexic errors. Additionally, 'TextHelp' has a word prediction feature that can predict a word from the context of the sentence giving up to ten options from a drop-down menu. Often dyslexic students have a word finding difficulty and this feature can therefore be very useful. This software also has a 'word wizard' that provides the user with a definition of any word; options regarding homophones; an outline of a phonic map and a talking help file.

'Inspiration'

'Inspiration' is a software programme to help the student develop ideas and organize thinking. Through the use of diagrams it helps the student comprehend concepts and information. Essentially the use of diagrams can help to make creating and modifying concept maps and ideas easier. The user can also prioritize and rearrange ideas, helping with essay writing. 'Inspiration' can therefore be used for brainstorming, organizing, pre-writing, concept mapping, planning and outlining. There are 35 inbuilt templates and these can be used for a range of subjects including English, History and Science. Dyslexic people often think in pictures rather than words. This technique can be used for note taking, for remembering information and organizing ideas for written work. The 'Inspiration' programme converts this image into a linear outline.

Strategies and suggestions for the teacher

Instructions to students

Children with dyslexia may very easily misunderstand or forget instructions that are given to them. It is important, therefore, that the teacher ensures that dyslexic children have understood the instructions before embarking on a task. Some suggestions for the teacher are shown below:

♦ give one instruction at a time;

♦ keep instructions short;

♦ preferably demonstrate what the task or instruction entails;

♦ if the child has written the instructions check that he/she understands what they have written.

Copying

Often children with dyslexia can have difficulty in copying accurately, particularly from the board. Copying long pieces of information should be avoided and if this is unavoidable the information should be subdivided into sections. Certainly the child will very likely take longer to copy information and extra time should be allowed for this. It will very likely be easier for the child to copy from a page or book that is positioned next to him/her, but again this may still be quite difficult.

Notetaking

Notetaking can be challenging for children with dyslexia. This can be due to a number of reasons:

♦ speed of processing, their actual writing may be slow and hesitant;

♦ they may feel the need to self-correct as they are taking down notes and may well make frequent mistakes in copying notes;

♦ they may have difficulty in identifying the key points and this can lead to copying notes that may be unnecessary and irrelevant;

♦ they may be poorly organized and the notes can be written without proper planning or organization.

These difficulties can be overcome by:

♦ providing a framework for writing notes, indicating the key points;

♦ providing typed notes on the key points;

♦ allowing plenty time for notetaking and preparation of written work;

♦ allowing notes to be wordprocessed.

Reading

Below are some teaching strategies to help with reading.

♦ Paired reading and peer tutoring (see Chapter 6). These strategies can be useful because the child obtains feedback and support from either an adult or from peers.

♦ Allow time to re-read – this is essential as often children with dyslexia have to read once for accuracy and a second time for comprehension.

♦ Teach reading in a multisensory manner using visual, auditory, kinesthetic and tactile stimulation.

♦ Provide opportunities for overlearning so that the child can use the word he/she is learning in as many different ways as possible.

♦ It is important that the child has at least Foundation skills in phonics and letter sounds but this should not be taught to the exclusion of meaning and language experience in context. This is particularly important as the child progresses through school. Most phonic programmes are aimed at younger children. Students who have only mastered the fundamentals of phonics can learn to read through language experience through what is known as top-down approaches. This involves the use of meaning and context as the start-ing point, rather than the individual decoding of words.

♦ It is best to utilize a range of reading materials and programmes and not focus exclusively on one approach.

♦ Taped books can be useful but they do need teacher input to ensure the child has appropriate under-standing of the narrative.

♦ It is best to use books that the child has selected and are based on his/her interests.

♦ When providing written notes or instructions it is a good idea to intersperse these with visuals.

♦ Larger print can be useful and the use of coloured backgrounds.

Spelling

Spelling can be very difficult for the dyslexic child because it involves many different cognitive skills such as memory, motor skills, writing accuracy, speed, visual skills and meaning. Spelling in context can be even more challenging as the child may be focusing on the meaning aspect of the piece he/she is writing and the child's attention may be predominantly on this. Spelling may be more erratic in a piece of prose as opposed to single word spelling, as in some spelling tests.

Below are some strategies for teaching spelling.

♦ Paired and peer spelling. Again this can provide a good model for spelling and reinforcement.

♦ Develop a spelling notebook with words that the child usually misspells. It is a good idea to use this in conjunction with the meaning of the words.

♦ Practice at writing and obtaining feedback on spelling.

♦ The use of a wordprocessor with a spellcheck – this can allow the child to note his/her spelling errors and insert these into their own spelling notebook.

♦ Spelling strategies such as look, cover, write and check.

Creative writing

Children with dyslexia have the potential to be very productive in creative writing. Often they have a good imagination and therefore can develop some interesting storylines. Often, however, this potential does not materialize. They can be thwarted from showing their real potential in creative writing by factors such as grammar, difficulty with structure and sequence and not being able to generate relevant details in the right order. One method that can be used to overcome this is the use of writing frames. David Wray, from the University of Warwick, has developed a number of strategies that can promote expressive writing, including writing frames. Two examples below show how they work.

Argument

I think that _____ because _____.
The reasons for my thinking this are, firstly _____.
Another reason is _____.
Moreover _____because _____
_____.

These (facts/arguments/ideas) show that _____.
Some people think that _____ because they argue that _____.

Discussion

Another group who agree with this point of view are

_____.
They say that _____.
On the other hand _____
disagree with the idea that _____.
They claim that _____.
They also say _____.
My opinion is _____
because _____.

(Adapted from David Wray's website:
www.warwick.ac.uk/staff/D.J.Wray/Ideas/frames.html)

Wray also shows how the following can be used in writing frames: Contrast, Comparison, Persuasion, Sequence. This type of strategy can be very useful for children with dyslexia.

Self-esteem

Self-esteem is one of the most crucial aspects of successful learning. A positive self-esteem is essential and this definitely applies to children with dyslexia. Success and positive feedback are necessary in order to develop and enhance a child's self-esteem. It is important that children with dyslexia feel they are succeeding and are valued. It can be quite challenging for the teacher to ensure this happens but there are a number of strategies that can be used. Below are some examples.

- ◆ Programmes such as Circle Time (Mosley 1996) can help to develop good interpersonal relations among children and encourage them to identify positive elements in others in the class. In this way efforts are made to ensure that every child is seen as special.

- ◆ Praise and feedback. It is important that children with dyslexia receive praise and positive feedback. This in itself can be as worthwhile as the most costly resource. Positive feedback is in fact a resource and one that needs to be used appropriately.

- ◆ Achievable targets. Success is important for self-esteem and this can be obtained by the child realizing him/herself that success has been achieved. It is important, therefore, that the targets and the tasks that are set are achievable. In fact the principles of SMART targets can be a guide for setting targets for children with dyslexia. SMART is an acronym for Specific, Measurable, Achievable, Relevant and Timely (Lloyd and Berthelot 1992).

Praise and success leading to a positive self-concept can therefore be extrinsic, that is being generated by others – such as praise from the teacher, or intrinsic, that is when the child realizes that he/she has been successful and is able to apportion that success to him/herself. The latter is much more difficult for children with dyslexia because quite often success, particularly in literacy subjects, can be difficult to achieve. There is, however, a great deal of evidence to highlight the importance of a positive self-concept for learning.

Summary of Chapter 3

This chapter has provided an overview of some teaching approaches and strategies that can be used for children with dyslexia. There are many commercial teaching programmes for dyslexia and each will have some merit. The key point is that specific programmes need to be complemented with the curricular work that is going on in the class. No programme by itself will provide the answer to dyslexia. This chapter has emphasized that point by providing some principles for teaching children with dyslexia, such as multisensory sequential objectives and the use of overlearning to help to achieve automaticity in learning.

This chapter also outlined some of the established programmes and approaches that can be used as well as the importance of using new technologies. There is considerable scope in ICT for supporting children and young people with dyslexia and new software programmes are constantly being developed. This can hold the promise of a more successful future for dyslexic children.

The chapter also provided some suggestions for teachers in giving instructions to students, notetaking, copying, reading and spelling, as well as the use of writing frames to help facilitate creative writing.

The teaching approaches and strategies outlined in this chapter can all help in some way to make education and literacy less of an ordeal for children with dyslexia. For that reason, the chapter concluded with reference to self-esteem. It is crucial that every effort is made to ensure that children with dyslexia can develop a positive self-esteem. This will help them overcome current and future barriers that may confront them as they seek to become proficient in literacy and in learning.

4

Curriculum Planning and Differentiated Approaches

It is important to recognize that specific teaching approaches, such as those described in the previous chapter, can be very useful for children with dyslexia, but equally, successful intervention may lie in curriculum planning and differentiation. Planning for learning is essential for all children and particularly important for dyslexic children. This chapter will therefore focus on curriculum planning, differentiation and the development of Individual Education Plans (IEPs).

Planning for learning

Planning for learning implies that it is necessary to consider the child's individual needs. For children with dyslexia this means that as much information as possible should be gathered in order to ensure that appropriate plans are developed.

Planning for learning involves consideration of factors relating to:

♦ the individual child and his/her profile based on a recent assessment;

♦ the learning environment;

♦ the needs and proposed targets and achievements envisaged;

♦ the resources and materials that are necessary;

♦ any additional specialist advice that is available (some of this can be web based – see Chapter 6).

Curriculum plans need to include an overall long-term programme as well as short-term targets. It is important to take a global view of the learner and not merely focus on specific individual targets or areas that need to be developed. This is particularly important in the case of dyslexia as dyslexic children usually have a weakness in reading accuracy and this difficulty can often dominate a curriculum and learning plan for that child. If this happens it can be to the detriment of other educational areas and indeed educational priorities such as thinking skills, comprehension and the development of language concepts.

In practice some of the general strategies that are adopted include:

♦ reducing content coverage of the curriculum to release more time for other areas of the curriculum in which the child shows some difficulties;

♦ relying on alternative means such as Information and Communication Technology;

♦ providing different curriculum content and specific materials or specialist teaching.

These practices noted above, however, have to be treated with caution as they can sometimes restrict, though not always, the child's education and curriculum access.

Cowne (2000) notes a number of important points for teachers planning intervention for individual pupils. These include:

♦ relating the principal curriculum objectives for pupils to overall school schemes;

♦ considering the way in which the principal objectives and key concepts are to be assessed in each subject area, the criteria that can indicate a satisfactory level of skills and how to record the outcome of the assessment;

♦ identifying the prerequisite skills that the child needs, including the prior level of knowledge required to understand any of the key concepts in the curriculum area;

♦ awareness of the existing skills and knowledge of the dyslexic child so that any necessary 'pre-teaching', or differentiated resource can be identified;

♦ considering ways in which various kinds of group work, with or without additional assistance from adults, might assist learning;

♦ considering the extent to which the key concepts in every subject area and lesson can be achieved and to set achievable objectives.

Reading policies

Schools will have general reading policies and these are necessary to ensure that literacy has a high profile in the school. It is important that such reading policies include provision and resources for children who may lag behind in some, but not all, aspects of literacy. This is the situation for children with dyslexia, who may have difficulty accessing print in terms of decoding and accuracy but can have a good understanding of language and the storyline in a narrative. It is important that they are able to access literature and stories even though their reading age may be below the reading age of the text. Reading needs to be seen as much more than 'cracking the code'. The meaning, inferences inherent in the text and social factors and customs that can be transmitted by text need to be emphasized.

The notion of critical literacy is an important factor to consider when developing a reading policy and curriculum plan. Critical literacy is associated with a broader view of reading that suggests the reader must be able to comprehend the meanings encoded by the author of the text, including those meanings that are not explicitly stated by the writer. This means the reader has to use inferences to establish what the writer is implying. This is a higher order thinking skill that is within the grasp of many children and young people with dyslexia. But the lack of access to print can often prevent this skill being utilized. It is for this reason that a general reading policy should contain elements and opportunities that can cater for the diverse needs of all students. It is also important to consider that not all children with dyslexia will show the same literacy profile, and again the individual needs of the student will have to be considered.

It has been suggested (Medwell 1995) that the literacy needs of all students should be considered in the development of school policies for reading. Medwell suggests that:

- we need to recognize that there is no one method of teaching and that different children may need different approaches;
- literacy involves creating the right environment in class, both in terms of organization of resources and of time;
- reading with a supportive adult is at the centre of reading instruction;
- assessment for formative and diagnostic purposes as well as statutory assessment is the basis of teaching and must be continuous and systematic;
- all children need to learn to use reading strategies, like skimming and scanning, and not have a total reliance on reading every word.

It can be noted from the above that reading, and a reading policy, needs to be seen as a whole-school intervention. This means that the diversity necessary to ensure that the needs of all children with dyslexia are met is a whole-school responsibility and therefore as much a management issue as it is a teacher obligation.

Barriers to learning

There are a number of barriers to learning that can prevent children and young people with dyslexia from progressing in the school curriculum. These barriers can be placed into the following categories:

- the curriculum;
- the task;
- the learner;
- the classroom and learning environment.

These factors can become barriers to learning if:

- there is not sufficient differentiation in the tasks;
- the pace is too fast;
- the child's base line is not fully appreciated;
- the child's skills are not fully recognized;
- insufficient attention is paid to the child's learning style;
- teaching approaches are inappropriate;
- the child's self-esteem is low;
- the materials are not motivating;
- the child is not equipped with strategies to overcome some of his/her difficulties, such as memory and organizational difficulties.

It is crucial that attention is paid to the needs of the learner and the learner's own perceptions of school and his/her learning experiences.

Student perceptions

Thompson and Chinn (2001) asked a group of adolescents attending a Maths and dyslexia summer school what hindered learning for them. The responses included the following:

♦ teachers who go too fast and expect too much;

♦ being expected to produce the same amount of work (as non-dyslexic pupils) in a given time;

♦ teachers who don't stick to the point;

♦ teachers who know I'm dyslexic but don't help me enough;

♦ being patronized;

♦ too much copying off the board and dictating notes;

♦ rubbing work off the board too soon;

♦ having test results read out loud;

♦ people who make fun of me, or who are sarcastic;

♦ being told off when I'm asking a friend for help;

♦ not being allowed to use my laptop in lessons;

♦ confusing 'dyslexic' with 'stupidity';

♦ lack of empathy for dyslexia;

♦ being made to read aloud in class.

It can be noted from the above that learners with dyslexia can be very sensitive to their learning experience. This needs to be borne in mind. The same research study also asked students what particular aspects about the learning experience had helped them. Their responses are shown below:

- help being given discreetly (and quietly) to individuals;

- being given more time;

- handouts with summaries of work;

- marking work in dark colours tidily and praise being given;

- working in smaller groups;

- teachers who care;

- grades that show individual improvement;

- marking that is clear and helpful;

- work judged for content not spelling.

These statements above are very revealing and show that emotional factors need to be considered as well as progress in literacy. This emphasizes the importance of self-esteem and self-belief. In a very revealing audio for a course for teachers on literacy and dyslexia, a student at a school for dyslexic children (The Red Rose School), when asked 'what was different about the school' answered 'that the teachers here make me believe in myself, that I can do it' (OU *Course materials E 801* 2002). Indeed, one of the key roles for teachers in relation to dyslexia is exactly that – to help the student to believe in him/herself.

Differentiation

Differentiation has been described as the action necessary to respond to the individual's requirements for curriculum access. It is important that *curriculum access* is not confused with *curriculum simplification*. They are not the same. Children with dyslexia may need support to achieve access to the same curriculum as others in the class, but once these supports are provided they can be as capable as achieving higher order thinking and learning skills as others in the year group. One of the key aspects in relation to differentiation is how the curriculum is presented and the teaching approaches. This means that differentiation:

♦ will affect the way the teacher delivers the curriculum;

♦ will determine the materials used;

♦ will influence the organizational structure within the learning context;

♦ will influence the expectations placed on the pupil.

Differentiation is not about a 'watered down' curriculum, but about making learning accessible to all.

Types of differentiation

Differentiation can be achieved through the following three ways.

Task
This means looking carefully at the tasks that are set and identifying the barriers within that task that can prevent dyslexic children from succeeding with the task. Below are some points to consider.

- Vocabulary.

- Sentence structure.

- Length of task instructions.

- How does the task relate to the child's previous knowledge?

- Is there sufficient guidance in the task instructions to ensure the child will be able to use previous knowledge?

- Can the task be provided in different ways, for example, visually?

- Is there guidance on how much time the child should spend on the task?

- Can the task be divided into steps to help the child achieve it?

- Is the reading level of the task consistent with the child's reading level.

- The resources to support the task should be well designed and the instructions on when and how to use additional resources should be clear.

- The provision of key words that the student may need to complete the task should be noted.

- Specialized vocabulary spelling lists that relate to the task should also be provided.

- A variety of tasks should be provided so that the child can access the task best suited to his/her abilities and prior understanding.

Teaching
This implies that how the lesson is taught and the curriculum delivered are important elements. The key elements include:

♦ ensuring there are opportunities for the child to work with groups, do individual work, peer tutoring and receive necessary one-to-one with the teacher;

♦ acknowledge the learning styles of students and appreciate that within a class there will be a range of learning styles.

Outcome
It is important to consider the product of learning and how the effect of learning is to be measured. Since the inception of formal education there has been a preoccupation with measuring performance through formal tests. While this method may yield some significant information, it may not be the best method for children with dyslexia. Although the examination system is not likely to change dramatically, there has been significant developments in the provision of supports for children with dyslexia. These include extra time and the use of a scribe and reader. Furthermore, there is evidence of examination boards consulting with dyslexia groups to ensure that examination questions will not be misunderstood by dyslexic students. The philosophy of dyslexia-friendly teaching has penetrated, particularly in the UK, into every sector of educational provision. Other means that can ensure that dyslexic children are considered in relation to task and learning outcome include:

71

♦ providing a range of possible outcomes from the task by encouraging children to present their work in a variety of ways, such as through the use of multi-media including tapes, videos and ICT;

♦ the use of coursework as an integral and continuous form of assessment;

♦ placing emphasis on practical skills, oral pres-entations and fieldwork as legitimate forms of assessment.

Individual Education Plans

Individual Education Plans (IEPs) are, in some coun-tries, seen as essential in planning interventions to meet the educational needs of children with dyslexia. Irrespective of the legislative requirements of the country an IEP is a valuable tool for ensuring the needs of the child with dyslexia are more carefully consid-ered. An IEP requires consultation between profes-sionals and, very importantly, between professionals and parents. This ensures that all involved in the child's education – teachers, psychologists and school man-agement, as well as parents, are involved. Depending on the age of the child, he/she should also be involved. There is some evidence, and a tendency, for IEPs to be vague and general – this is unfortunate and inappropri-ate. IEPs should contain specific short-term targets as well as medium- and long-term goals.

Tod (2002) identifies a number of principles for schools to use to evaluate the development of IEPs for students who are experiencing difficulties in literacy. Some of these principles are summarized below.

♦ Clarity of purpose – an IEP should have clear aims for individual pupils and these aims should be seen as part of whole-school planning and provision.

♦ Target setting – targets should reflect high expectations as well as the need to develop social and academic aspects of learning; address skills and strategies, and build on pupil strengths.

♦ Proactive – it is important that IEPs support early identification of literacy difficulties and trigger proactive planning.

♦ Resourcing – it is important that IEPs harness and support efficient use of resources and reflect collaborative educational effort.

The content of IEPs will differ depending on the age and level of the child. It is important, however, that the short- medium- and long-term goals are clearly expressed and that there is provision within the IEP for monitoring and revision. IEPs clearly generate additional work for teachers, particularly administrative and record keeping. However, the reflective benefits of IEPs, which by their very nature encourage teachers to obtain an overview of the child's educational needs and planning of intervention, is invaluable.

Learning styles

A child's learning style is an important determinant of successful learning. This applies to all learners, but it has considerable significance for learners who may find aspects of the curriculum challenging, such as dyslexic learners. Learning styles can help the child develop confidence in learning and eventually help him/her become an autonomous learner where they can tackle a task independently of others. Knowledge of learning styles is therefore beneficial for the teacher and important for the child.

A definition of learning styles is shown below (adapted from Keefe 1987).

Learning styles are characteristic learning preferences that are usually stable indicators of how the learner interacts with a task or stimuli. This can be influenced by previous learning, the nature of the task and the learning environment. Considerations of individual learning styles will promote more effective and independent learning.

The learning styles research suggests that consideration of learning styles within teaching programmes and the curriculum can help students 'learn how to learn' and that 'at risk' students such as those weak in analytic and discrimination skills can learn to control their learning and thus process information more efficiently and effectively.

Some pointers to providing for the child's learning style are shown below.

♦ Acknowledge the student's preferred learning style – visual, auditory, kinesthetic or tactile when presenting material.

♦ Present information in small units so that the child can experiment with different ways of tackling the task.

♦ Use a range of materials that can incorporate visual, auditory, kinesthetic and tactile preferences.

♦ Key points should be presented at the initial stage of learning new material.

♦ Discuss with the child **how** he or she tackled a task.

♦ Ask children how they prefer to study at home.

♦ Observe how children work when given a free hand, for example do they work in groups, alone, ask a lot of questions, or refer to books?

♦ Consider the importance of the environment such as light, design, seating arrangements and the level of noise when planning for a child's learning style. Some children may prefer a quiet environment while others may prefer some background noise or some type of music.

A dyslexic style?

It is important to acknowledge that dyslexic children are individuals and it is wrong to suggest that all children with dyslexia will have the same style. Due to the nature of the difficulties associated with dyslexia – which tend to affect left hemisphere-type skills such as decoding, language and remembering detail – dyslexic children and adults would tend to have a right hemisphere preference. This means they would likely be:

♦ visual and kinesthetic;

♦ prefer working in an informal learning environment;

Dyslexia

♦ like background noise or music;

♦ prefer to work in groups with a lot of interaction;

♦ prefer short tasks with frequent breaks.

It is important, however, to identify each child's style on an individual basis as the example with Tom, aged 13, below shows. This involves an interview with a learner in relation to a task involving reading a passage and answering questions about it.

> Firstly I read the passage which is okay for me because I am now a good reader. I then identified all the words with 'ck' sound and underlined these words, then checked that I had not missed any. My next task was to write 8 words ending in 'cket' – well I knew the first one was 'rocket' which I read in the passage. I then thought of some words which rhymed with rocket such as 'sprocket' and made a list with these.

There are a number of important points to emerge from this example above. First, Tom was aware of how to tackle this particular task. When asked how he did it he was able to respond immediately and fully, so he was aware of the process he used. This implies that he would be able to use this process with other similar tasks. Some children with dyslexia are not aware of the processes they use to obtain certain responses. Tom in fact was very aware of his own style.

It is very common for children with dyslexia to start tasks with a visual stimuli, even, if they may have as Tom has, an analytic preference.

Below are the key points relating to learning styles.

♦ Every effort should be made to organize the class-room environment in a manner which can be adapted to suit a range of styles.

♦ In classrooms where there are a number of dys-lexic learners, the environment would likely be global, which means the lighting, design and indeed the whole learning atmosphere, needs to be considered.

♦ It is also important that the teacher has an aware-ness of what is meant by learning styles and how to identify different styles in children.

♦ Although there are many different instruments that can be used, the teacher's observations and discus-sion with students while they are engaged on a task can be extremely beneficial.

♦ The experience of learning may be more important to children with dyslexia than the actual finished product.

♦ At the same time it is important that children with dyslexia themselves become aware of their own learning style. This is the first and most important step to achieving a degree of self-sufficiency in learning.

♦ Acknowledging learning styles, therefore, can help to promote skills that extend beyond school and can equip students with dyslexia for lifelong learning.

Summary of Chapter 4

This chapter has considered curriculum perspectives in dealing with dyslexia. This means that the following need to be considered in planning effective learning for children with dyslexia.

♦ Whole-school planning – it is important that dyslexia is seen as being a whole-school responsibility and that all teachers and management have an awareness of dyslexia.

♦ School policies – this chapter highlighted an example of the need for reading policies in schools and it is important that these policies should consider the curricular needs of children with dyslexia

♦ It is important to note the barriers to learning that children with dyslexia experience and to develop strategies through planning, provision and practice to help them overcome these barriers.

♦ The need to understand what is meant by differentiation is important. It does not mean a 'watered down' curriculum but a curriculum presented with diversity; acknowledging there are a variety of means of displaying competence in learning.

♦ An Individual Education Plan could and should provide an opportunity to develop and reflect on practice by identifying short-, medium- and long-term targets.

♦ It is important to consider the student's perceptions of learning and in particular the student's own learning style. It is necessary to identify this on an individual basis because although there may be similarities between children with dyslexia in relation to learning styles, it is important to perceive the child first and foremost as an individual learner.

5

Social and Emotional Considerations

Social and emotional factors are of paramount importance in education and particularly in the current trend, now evident in most countries, of inclusive schooling. In the thrust towards inclusion, curriculum access and attainment targets, the need to consider the child's social and emotional wellbeing can be overlooked. Yet social and emotional considerations can enhance the child's self-concept and self-esteem and this in turn can promote effective learning. It is vitally important to consider this for children with dyslexia as often they have experienced some kind of failure after only a few years in school. Once a child has experienced failure it is very difficult to reverse this process. The cycle of learned helplessness can be quite common among children with dyslexia. This cycle suggests that a child who has difficulty in learning, or in the case of dyslexic children, in reading, can easily become switched off from learning and the 'can't do' becomes 'won't do'.

What are the social and emotional considerations that can help children with dyslexia? These can be divided into school, community and home.

Factors that can help develop social and emotional confidence

School factors

There are programmes that help with understanding the needs of others such as Circle Time and social education activities. These activities involve turn taking, decision making, understanding different cultures and disabilities, and anti-bullying activities. These can promote an understanding of equity and help children understand individual differences and diversity in cultures. Activities such as these can promote self-understanding and self-confidence. Additionally, such programmes can provide an enhanced understanding of society in general and promote tolerance and understanding within the wider school community.

Community factors

These could be participation in community groups and clubs and dyslexia-friendly libraries. These can promote reading and literature in an non-threatening manner. There are also opportunities within the community for reading projects involving local newspapers and other community organizations. These can promote a positive view of reading and this can bolster the self-esteem of children with dyslexia.

Below are two examples of community projects in reading.

Reading in Partnership Project – this project took place in Sunderland in the North East of England. The principal aim of the project was to increase the level of reading competence of all children in Year 3 at primary schools.

Throughout its existence the project developed a number of initiatives linked to the community. This involved schemes to encourage parents and children to read together. One such scheme involved the active participation of the local newspaper and another the local libraries. Another of the successes of the project was the encouragement of local volunteers to become involved with the schools.

This project successfully stimulated a community interest in reading and by doing so emphasized that literacy difficulties needed to be dealt with at an early age. The overall ethos of the project helped all children achieve some degree of success in literacy. Dyslexic children in particular benefited from this in terms of enhanced training of teaching staff, additional resources, developing links between home and school and early intervention. This type of initiative clearly helped to minimize the effects of literacy difficulties.

Literacy Collaborative – a literacy collaborative project that took place in the mid-1990s in Newcastle provides a good example of the importance of links between school and the community in relation to literacy. This project was a community-based initiative and a joint collaboration between the Newcastle City Council and the Newcastle Library Trust and aimed to raise standards and promote literacy for enjoyment and achievement in the Newcastle area. The collaborative organized community reading and writing events for all ages, including creative writing projects, additional support to schools to foster work with parents, and in-service education for Newcastle education authority staff. There was liaison with youth and community workers to ensure that literacy was not just a school-based task, but one which can provide fun and enjoyment after school.

Home factors

Positive reinforcement at home is essential for the child with dyslexia. Sometimes this can be difficult as it is easy for parents to compare a child's progress with siblings or with other school friends. It is important to recognize that children do progress at different rates and that they will show differing abilities in different types of tasks. It will be inappropriate to compare children in this way and comparing children with other children can be quite damaging for young people with dyslexia. The role of parents is very important in this respect and this will be discussed in more detail in the following chapter. It is sufficient, however, to acknowledge that the social and emotional development of dyslexic children is not totally the school's responsibility and that the positive reinforcement a child can receive from home can help to provide positive self-esteem and motivation even though he/she may be struggling with literacy at school.

Children's perceptions and self-esteem

It is worthwhile emphasizing that a child's perception of reading is an important element in how successful and motivated he/she will be with reading. One of the most successful means of motivating children to read is to ensure that the reading material is age appropriate, culturally appropriate and of interest to the child. It is interesting to consider the National Foundation for Educational Research figures in the box below that show the most popular books for children in the 9 to 10 age range.

Top ten books children like to read (scores in per cent)	
Ghost/horror/supernatural	45
Magazines	40
Joke books	32
Sport	28
Adventure stories	27
Animal stories	21
Comics	21
School stories	16
Mystery	16
Fairy tales	16

Although this study was conducted just before the Harry Potter series of books were published, it does in part explain why the series made a huge impact among children. In the study above horror/supernatural stories surpass even popular magazines. This emphasizes that it is important to ask the child, or provide opportunities for individual selection of books of the child's own choice. This is one of the main aspects of paired reading, where it is crucial the child chooses his/her own reading material.

Perceptions of reading

How do children perceive reading? This question was put to a sample of children aged between 7 and 10 years by the author and the responses illustrate the different perceptions and beliefs children hold of reading. Some of the responses include:

♦ learning words

♦ learning new words

♦ looking at words and saying them

♦ learning about things

♦ finding out about things

♦ stories

♦ words and sentences

♦ school work

♦ pleasing the teacher!

The main distinction that can be drawn from the responses relate to aspects of the **task** of reading, rather than the **function**. Those who focused on the 'task' highlighted aspects such as the decoding of words and the learning of these words. A typical response from the 'task' group was 'reading is when you look at words and you say them in your mind'. The 'function' group recognized reading as an activity from which they derived pleasure and the purpose of reading was to obtain meaning from text. Quite often children with dyslexia would fit into the former category.

Why do children perceive reading in such different ways? Does the answer to this question lie in the method and strategy used to teach children reading? Or perhaps the answer to this is related more to the child's skills and abilities and how easy and accessible learning to read is for the child. If the child perceives reading as an arduous exercise and a product of classroom routine and relentless practice, then reading will be perceived by the child in a less than positive manner. If this is the child's perception of reading, then the real meaning of reading is lost.

Children with dyslexia seldom have a perception of reading that reveals the pleasure of books and the real meaning of print. They often perceive reading as a dreaded exercise, that requires skills in precision and accuracy and quite often this is very challenging for them. This presents a challenge for teachers. That challenge is how to teach the basic fundamental structure and framework for the understanding of print and at the same time providing an enriched and meaningful language experience to facilitate and encourage access to books. This can help the child gain some real appreciation of the message and pleasure of books.

Perceptions of school

When children with dyslexia were asked about their feelings on school (Johnson 2004), nearly one third of the responses related to feeling stupid or different and not knowing as much as the others. Some of the comments made by the children are shown below.

You have to ask for spellings all the time if you want to get them right and the teacher writes them on the board which makes the rest of the class think how stupid I am.

Not being given credit for being as intelligent as others just because I have difficulty in speed of writing and spelling.

I am never picked to do cool things because I can't read or remember things like everyone else.

When the researchers asked, 'If you were able to tell all teachers something about how to teach pupils with dyslexia' there was a clear consensus among the pupils. More than 8 out of 10 said that teachers should explain better in the first place, and then check whether pupils had understood. They should be prepared to repeat instructions and explanations. 'Talk plainly, clearly and to the child.' 'Watch over my shoulder every so often and write spellings in the margin.' 'Concentrate on what the person is saying without thinking about what you are going to have for dinner or who's fighting over there. They are having a hard time telling the teacher because they are embarrassed.' 'They should explain what you have to do as many times as needed – twice the same way before maybe a different approach.'

The important point to consider about this study is that dyslexic pupils' views are important and need to be heard. This emphasizes the importance of boosting the child's self-concept to ensure that he/she has a positive view of school and of school work. There are many different methods, and indeed programmes, aimed at boosting self-esteem and all will be of some benefit. Some general pointers to enhancing self-esteem are shown below.

♦ **Praise** – lots of it, but it should be appropriate as the child will recognize if the praise is in any way insincere. This highlights the need to ensure that the learning targets that are set are achievable and then praise can legitimately be given.

♦ **Feedback** – providing constructive pointers on how an improvement can be made and noting the good points about the piece of work.

♦ **Responsibility** – giving the child some responsibility for some aspects of classroom organization, for example, being in charge of the pens or some other duty that is very manageable for the child.

♦ **Success** – this cannot be understated, as success is the most influential factor in self-esteem. Success does not have to be in reading, but if it is that would be even more effective. But the child can experience success just by completing work and by participating effectively in small groups.

♦ **Peer approval** – what others in the class 'think' of a child is very important to that child. Children need approval, and approval and friendship from peers is very likely to be more influential than from adults. It is important to ensure that the class is aware of the needs of others and can consider the need to be positive towards other children in the class.

♦ **Understanding** – it is important that children with dyslexia have some self-understanding of dyslexia and how it affects them. This need not be negative and the positive aspects of dyslexia should be high-lighted. It should be mentioned that there are some very famous and successful individuals with dyslexia who have achieved success, such as Richard Branson, Tom Cruise and Jackie Stewart. It is worth spending some time with the child with dyslexia to explain to them what dyslexia is and how strategies can be developed to overcome any of the difficulties associated with dyslexia.

Reflections on experiences – people with dyslexia

Some accounts of people with dyslexia who have had to overcome many challenges before finding success are shown below (adapted from Reid and Kirk 2001).

'I had a sort of mixed school experience; to begin with I enjoyed school but later when I moved to a different town I felt I was not accepted by teachers and some other chil-dren. This made things quite difficult for me and at times I felt quite threatened. My dyslexic difficulties were not identified at school but I was taken out to a remedial class several times for extra tuition. It was my father who noticed that I was not reading accurately – he noted that when he mistakenly turned two pages of my reader I con-tinued reading what I thought should be on the page – I was clearly reading for context and did not realize that two pages had been turned by mistake. Perhaps looking back I felt I was probably forgotten about at school – perhaps the problem was that I was not able to say what I wanted to say. I was often reluctant to be involved in discussion in case I made a fool of myself.'

Dyslexia

'When I left school I was fortunate and managed to get an apprenticeship as a stone mason with a very small firm who did not ask me to attend any college course. On reflection I wish I had been motivated a bit more at school and that my dyslexic difficulties had been recognized. But at least now I have a second chance and also see myself as being more reliable and certainly more socially aware.'

'I was diagnosed as dyslexic when I was 31 and this has made a considerable difference to me. At school I had problems with Maths; I was totally unaware of what was going on in the classroom, I actually thought I had been away but I hadn't. This and my other difficulties, I now know were due to my dyslexia, and resulted in low self-confidence. With the coloured acetate I can read whole lines, it seems to relax my eyes and I can now read with comprehension.

This has given me a real boost and I have now passed many exams in counselling, learning support and child care. I will never stop learning – it is like a hunger and I want to go on – ideally I would like to become a special needs teacher.'

'I had a really horrendous school experience, I was in the bottom groups for English and Maths and this meant I was with children who were not interested in school and probably not very able. I was serious about my work but it was impossible to perform well in the class I was put into. I was bullied quite a bit and also given work that I knew was well below my capabilities. On two occasions I just felt I could not, and should not, have to cope with this and actually ran out of school. No one at that school bothered to investigate why I had difficulties, I was very good verbally.

Dyslexia was kind of loosely mentioned at primary school but the school did not take it any further.

At secondary school I failed virtually all my subjects except for art and science but I was even advised against doing art at college. Looking back I feel I was written off at school and this still has an effect on my self esteem.'
(Vanessa on whom the above case study is based is now a successful artist.)

It can be seen from these accounts that all reflect on their school experiences and these reflections are less than positive. Although the people in the case studies above succeeded, their journey would have been much smoother had their self-esteem been boosted at school.

Summary of Chapter 5

This chapter has provided an overview of some of the key factors that can determine the development of a child's self-esteem. A positive self-esteem is crucial for children if they are to be successful learners and every effort needs to be made to ensure that every opportunity is taken to utilize classroom and other learning experiences to promote a positive self-esteem. This is particularly relevant for dyslexic children. Some of the key areas and suggestions indicated in this chapter are listed below.

♦ The need to promote a positive self-esteem early in the child's education in order to avoid the unfortunate situation that can occur with 'learned helplessness', which can be demotivating and demoralizing for the child.

♦ The use of community supports such as libraries and other organizations in order to ensure that there is a wider awareness and a good understanding of dyslexia in the wider community.

♦ The importance of children's perceptions of reading and the need to ensure that they can maintain a positive view of reading and of the purpose of books.

♦ Similarly, there is a need, particularly among children with dyslexia, to ensure that they can have a positive view of school. It is important that areas of strengths are identified, as dyslexic children can often have abilities in different areas and identifying these areas can help develop a positive attitude to school.

♦ Praise and appropriate and positive feedback are essential and reinforces the need to embark on programmes such as Circle Time. This can help children appreciate the needs of others and interact with others in the class in a positive way.

♦ The chapter concluded with some reflections from dyslexic people who had been through varied experiences at school and college, some very negative, on account of their dyslexia. Their comments on how they overcame these difficulties provide encouragement to others.

♦ The chapter essentially suggests that a positive self-esteem can be instrumental in helping dyslexic children deal with their difficulties and this needs to be considered as complementary to intervention programmes in literacy.

6

Information for Parents and Teachers

Parents

There is no doubt that parents have a key role to play in the social, emotional and educational development of children with dyslexia. Parents can have an important role in the initial identification of dyslexia as often they may spot signs of dyslexia while the child is still very young.

Parents may note that one child in the family may take longer to learn the alphabet, may be more reluctant to read than others in the family, may be more forgetful, may be even a bit more clumsy. Many of these things can be quite normal and merely highlight the normal individual differences between children – even children in the same family. It is also important that parents and schools work with each other effectively. The child is usually the first to pick up any disagreement between the school and home and the research suggests this can have a negative effect on the child.

Some possible factors that may prompt concern are listed below, but it is important to note that this list is not exhaustive and much depends on the individual child's stage of development. This is particularly important in younger children as many of the signs of dyslexia can in fact be an early phase of the normal developmental process in children.

Pre-school

Parents may raise some concern if some of the following are present:

♦ forgetfulness

♦ speech difficulty

♦ reversal of letters

♦ difficulty remembering letters of the alphabet

♦ difficulty remembering the sequence of letters of the alphabet

♦ if there is a history of dyslexia in the family

♦ coordination difficulties, e.g. bumping into tables and chairs

♦ difficulties with tasks which require fine motor skills, such as tying shoelaces

♦ slow at reacting to some tasks

♦ reluctance to concentrate on a task for a reasonable period of time

♦ confusing words which sound similar.

School age

♦ reluctance to go to school

♦ signs of not enjoying school

- reluctance to read

- difficulty learning words and letters

- difficulty with phonics (sounds)

- poor memory

- coordination difficulties

- losing items

- difficulty forming letters

- difficulty copying

- difficulty colouring

- poor organization of materials.

Support at home

It is important to appreciate that school can be quite an exhausting experience for children with dyslexia. They are constantly being asked to undertake activities they find challenging and may tire easily when faced with these daily challenges. Home, therefore, should not be a 'second' school but a supportive environment. At the same time there are activities that can be done at home to reinforce the learning taking place at school.

- Some reading programmes such as *Toe by Toe* can be carried out in the home as the programme does not require any specialist training.

- Reading schemes usually have follow up readers and these can be used at home.

♦ Paired Reading can also be carried out very successfully at home as it is based on the parent and the child reading together. Keith Topping from 'The Centre for Paired Learning' suggests that paired reading is a very successful method and involves the parent (tutor) and the child (tutee) reading aloud at the same time. It is, however, a specific structured technique. Both parent and child read all the words out together with the parent modulating their speed to match that of the child, while giving a good model of competent reading. The child must read every word and when the child says a word wrong, the parent just tells the child the correct way to say the word, the child then repeats the word correctly and the pair continue reading. Saying 'no' and giving phonic and other prompts is forbidden. However, parents do not jump in and correct the child straight away. The rule is the parents pause and give the child four or five seconds to see if they will put it right by themselves.

It is intended only for use with individually chosen, highly motivating, non-fiction or fiction books that are **above** the independent readability level of the child. One of the important aspects of paired reading and indeed any reading activities is praise – the parent should look pleased when the child succeeds using this technique.

♦ Discussion is also a good reinforcing vehicle. It is important for parents to find out what their child is doing in History or Geography as the content of many topics in these subjects can be incorporated into family outings or discussions. For example, a family trip in the car can be used to reinforce some historical landmarks or the names of crops grown in the area. Similarly, a visit to a castle, museum or art gallery can all reinforce names, events and experiences the child may have had in some of their school subjects.

♦ Reinforcement at home is particularly important for dyslexic children because they have a difficulty in automaticity. This means that even when they have learnt a new word or skill it may not be fully automatized. The implication of this is that they may forget the word or skill after a short while, for example, during the school holiday, if it is not being used. Automaticity is achieved through practice and actually using the new word in as many different settings and ways as possible. The research indicates that dyslexic children take longer than others to achieve automaticity and therefore require overlearning in order to consolidate the new learning. Parents can do this at home or on family outings without necessarily referring to school work.

♦ Motivating children to read – this can be challenging since it may be difficult to find age appropriate reading material that is at the child's reading level. Series of books that emphasizes high interest and lower levels of vocabulary can be extremely useful. One such example are those from Barrington Stoke. This series of books have been written with the reluctant reader in mind and they can help dyslexic children of all ages with reading fluency, reading comprehension and developing processing speed (see page 109).

There is a great deal of information available and voluntary groups that can offer advice and support to parents. It is important that parents recognize that the school should be the first 'port of call' as often at least one member of staff will have some knowledge of dyslexia and the school may also have suitable resources for parents. A list of some useful organizations and websites, some of which can be appropriate for parents, appears later in this chapter.

Summary

This part of the chapter has emphasized the following:

♦ the need to encourage parents to play a key role in working with the school to support their dyslexic son/daughter;

♦ the suggestion that parents may recognize the symptoms of dyslexia, especially in young children, and this emphasizes the need for close liaison between home and school;

♦ parents can reinforce what is happening in school and can follow up reading activities carried out in school – it is important, however, to ensure that home does not become a 'second' school and a relaxed environment is necessary when the child is undertaking homework or other educational pursuits;

♦ to consider that children with dyslexia can easily become de-motivated with reading and with learning and every effort should be made to ensure that age appropriate reading material geared to the child's own interests is available.

General information and resources

The remainder of this chapter will describe some of the resources that can be accessed by teachers and in some cases also by parents. There is an increasing range of resources that can be used for dyslexia, and sometimes this can contribute to some confusion on what is the most appropriate resource. There is no easy answer to that, except that what works for one dyslexic child may not be effective for another child. It is important to consider the child's learning profile and learning style when selecting a resource. Some of the resources mentioned below are in the form of books and references that often form the core texts in training courses on dyslexia for teachers. This is an important point, as teachers at all levels need to engage in some sort of training in this area. There has been an increase in training courses on dyslexia and many of these courses are validated by a university or college and approved by national bodies such as the British Dyslexia Association in the UK.

Books and learning activities

♦ **Alpha to Omega Activity Packs** by Hornsby, Pool and Shear. These contain photocopiable worksheets to reinforce the alpha to omega reading programme.

♦ **Word Wasp** by Harry Cowling (West Yorkshire: Wasp Publications). This book teaches spelling rules and contains exercises for dyslexic children which can be used by parents and teachers.

♦ **Learning Can Be Fun** by Sue Briggs ((1999, second impression, 2001) Hertfordshire: Egon Publishers). This is a structured multisensory training pack for mainstream teachers wishing to improve their pupils' literacy skills using an active approach through games and exercises. The pack consists of an Introductory Book, Book 1 on alphabet sequencing and Book 2 on syllable division for word attack skills.

♦ **Specific Learning Difficulties: A Teacher's Guide** by Margaret Crombie ((1997) Northumberland: Ann Arbor Publishers). This book is a practical guide to all aspects of teaching and supporting a dyslexic pupil in the mainstream setting and can also be useful for parents.

♦ **Phonic Code Cracker** by Sylvia Russell ((1992, revised 2000) Glasgow: Jordanhill College Publications). This is a structured scheme which provides intensive phonic practice to assist in acquiring literacy skills.

♦ **Get Better Grades** by Magie Agnew, Steve Barlow, Lee Pascal and Steve Skidmore ((1995) London: Piccadily Press). This short text on study skills looks at attitude, organization, listening and notetaking, reading and writing skills and revision for examinations. The information is presented in an eye-catching manner and contains study strategies more suitable for older children and even some adults.

♦ **In the Mind's Eye: Visual Thinkers, Gifted People with Learning Difficulties, Computer Images and**

the Ironies of Creativity by Thomas G. West ((1997) New York: Prometheus Books). This text highlights the positive side of dyslexia. It provides extensive profiles of gifted people such as Faraday, Einstein and da Vinci who were all dyslexic, and examines patterns in creativity and relates these patterns to computers and visual images and the implications of these for dyslexic students and adults. There are some insights into the potential of the dyslexic learner, perhaps encapsulated in the statement: 'We ought to begin to pay less attention to getting everyone over the same hill using the same path. We may wish to encourage some to take different routes to the same end. Then we might see good reasons for paying careful attention to their descriptions of what they have found. We may wish to follow them some day.'

♦ **Quality Circle Time in the Primary Classroom** by Jenny Mosley ((1996) Cambridge: LDA). This book is a guide to enhancing self-esteem, self-discipline and positive relationships. It focuses on quality Circle Time in the classroom following on from the author's previous book *Turn Your School Around*.

The book is divided into five parts – part one on establishing positive relationships in the classroom; part two on creating a calm and positive classroom ethos; part three on exploring the use of Circle Time activities; part four on circle meetings; and part five provides further information on Circle Time, for example, how it can relate to the national curriculum.

This book is a very comprehensive guide to Circle Time activities and how the activities can be integrated and utilized within the school setting. It contains ideas and suggestions for further activity related to Circle Time and the programmes and activities are all underpinned by a circular model developed by the author showing how Circle Time can be implemented within the school system.

♦ **Dyslexia – Parents in Need** by Pat Heaton ((1996) London: Whurr Publishers). This book describes some of the responses from parents in answer to research questions affecting parents of dyslexic children. It deals with aspects such as early signs, language difficulties, parents' feelings and perceptions, practical aspects and factors influencing effective liaison with the school. Section two of the book contains activities, including over 20 pages of word searches and other game activities for identifying vowels and consonants.

♦ **Learning Styles: A Guide for Teachers and Parents** by Barbara Given and Gavin Reid ((1998) Lancashire: Red Rose Publications). This book provides insights into the five learning systems – emotional, social, cognitive, physical and reflective; and practical applications of learning styles. It also contains a description of an 'interactive observation checklist' developed by the authors, for identification of individual learning styles as well as a range of resources which can be utilized by the teacher to help identify and teach to the student's learning style. The book covers the full age range of students.

♦ **Dyslexia: A Practitioner's Handbook** (3rd edition) by Gavin Reid ((2003) Chichester: John Wiley and

Sons). This comprehensive handbook answers many important questions integrating research and practice in an accessible form. This practical guide aims to help professionals and parents make an informed choice in the selection of materials, and provides a choice of strategies for classroom use for teachers. The text explores and explains research in reading and learning, and promotes the use of learning styles and study skills techniques. The book contains a wealth of assessment techniques providing an assessment framework which teachers can implement and adapt to accommodate to their own particular teaching. It covers many learning approaches from early education to higher education.

♦ **Dyslexia in Adults: Education and Employment** by Gavin Reid and Jane Kirk ((2000) Chichester: John Wiley and Sons). This book is a comprehensive guide, that offers strategies and guidance on adult dyslexia within education, the workplace and everyday life, covering many questions and issues that in the past have gone unanswered. It includes moving accounts about adult dyslexics, assessment and teaching strategies, strengths and weaknesses, the role of the tutor and where to get additional help and information. Careful consideration has been given to layout, spacing, font, and so on, with plenty of subheadings helping to break down the information into bite-size pieces, making it easier to read, process and understand.

♦ **Listening and Literacy Index – A Group Test to Identify Specific Learning Difficulties** by Charles Weedon and Gavin Reid ((2001) London: Hodder

Murray). This comprises Test Forms, Teacher's Handbook and Specimen Set.

♦ **Dyslexia: A Complete Guide for Parents** by Gavin Reid ((2004) Chichester: John Wiley and Sons).

♦ **Dyslexia: Successful Inclusion in the Secondary School** by Lindsay Peer and Gavin Reid (eds) ((2001) London: David Fulton Publishers).

Websites

Dr Gavin Reid
www.gavinreid.co.uk

Dr. Loretta Giorcelli (well-known international consultant)
www.doctorg.org

Red Rose School
www.dyslexiacentre.com

Organizations

Adult Dyslexia Organization
www.futurenet.co.uk/charity/ado/index

Arts Dyslexia Trust
www.sniffout.net/home/adt

Creative Learning Company New Zealand
www.creativelearningcentre.com

Dyslexia Association of Ireland
www.acld-dyslexia.com

Dyslexia College
www.dyslexia-college.com
Information and resources about dyslexia for dyslexic students at college or university.

Dyslexia Institute
www.dyslexia-inst.org.uk

Dyslexia Online Magazine
www.dyslexia-parent.com/magazine

The British Dyslexia Association
www.bda-dyslexia.org.uk

The European Dyslexia Association
www.bedford.ac.uk/eda

Articles and reviews about dyslexia

Dyslexia North West
www.dyslexiacentre.com
Registered charity based at the Red Rose School.

Dyslexia Online Journal
www.dyslexia-adults.com/journal

Dyslexia Parents Resource
www.dyslexia-parent.com
Information and resources about dyslexia for parents of children who are, or may be, dyslexic.

Dyslexia Research Trust
www.dyslexic.org.uk
Current Research, Newsletter, Conferences, Publications Upcoming, Talks and Lectures.

Dyslexia Teacher
www.dyslexia-teacher.com
Information and resources about dyslexia for teachers of dyslexic children.

Dyslexia UK
www.dyslexia.uk.com
Site providing information and guidance on all topics relating to dyslexia.

European Dyslexia Academy for Research and Training (E-DART)
www.psyk.uu.se/edart

Family Onwards
www.familyonwards.com

Helen Arkell Dyslexia Centre
www.arkellcentre.org.uk

Hornsby International Dyslexia Centre
www.hornsby.co.uk

I am dyslexic
www.iamdyslexic.com
A site put together by an 11-year-old dyslexic boy.

Institute for Neuro-Physiological Psychology (INPP)
www.inpp.org.uk

Learning and Behaviour Charitable Trust New Zealand
www.lbctnz.co.nz

Mark College
www.markcollege.somerset.sch.uk

Mindroom
www.mind-room.org
A charity dedicated to spreading greater awareness and understanding of learning difficulties. Goal to achieve by the year 2020 that all children with learning difficulties in the UK are identified and helped.

PATOSS
www.patoss-dyslexia.org

Quantum Learning
www.trainthebrain.co.uk
Jonathan O'Brien, courses and publications on learning and studying.

School Daily
www.schooldaily.com
New Zealand-based up to date educational news and debate.

SNAP assessment
www.SNAPassessment.com

The Dyslexia Shop
www.thedyslexiashop.com

The International Dyslexia Association (IDA)
www.interdys.org
Formerly the Orton Dyslexia Society – largest dyslexia organisation in the world – branches in every state in the USA and international affiliates.

Tourette Scotland
www.tourettescotland.org

World Dyslexia Network Foundation
web.ukonline.co.uk/wdnf/advice
A series of advice and help sheets have been written by leading experts in their fields.

World of Dyslexia
www.worldofdyslexia.com
also www.dyslexia-parent.com/world of dyslexia for useful links.

Literacy

Centre for Early Literacy (University of Maine)
www.ume.maine.edu/~cel
Links to reading recovery project and literacy for primary children.

International Reading Organization
www.reading.org/about
American: bulletin boards, information on associations with links.

National Literacy Strategy
www.standards.dfes.gov.uk/literacy

Paired reading, writing and thinking (Keith Topping)
www.dundee.ac.uk/psychology/TRW

United Kingdom Reading Association
www.ukra.org
Newsletter, publications, and links worth looking at.

Governments

Department for Education and Skills (DfES)
www.dfes.gov.uk

Republic of Ireland
www.irlgov.ie/educ/publications/dyslexia

Scottish Executive
www.scotland.gov.uk/search2/search.asp

Publishers

Barrington Stoke
www.barringtonstoke.co.uk
Books for reluctant readers including teenage fiction.

Better Books
www.betterbooks.co.uk
3 Paganel Drive, Dudley DY1 4AZ

Buzan Centres Ltd.
www.Mind-Map.com
54 Parkstone Road, Poole, Dorset BH15 2PG

Crossbow Education
www.crossboweducation.com
41 Sawpit Lane, Stafford, Staffordshire ST17 OTE
Games for learning.

David Fulton
www.fultonpublishers.co.uk
The Chiswick Centre, 414 Chiswick High Road, London
W4 5TF

Easylearn
www.easylearn.co.uk
Trent House, Fiskerton, Southwell, Notts. NG25 OUH

Easy reader
www.easyreader.org.uk
4 White Hart Street, Thetford IP24 1AD

Hodder Murray
www.hoddertests.co.uk
338 Euston Road, London NW1 3BH

Iansyst Ltd.
www.dyslexic.com

John Wiley and Sons Ltd.
www.wiley.com

LDA
www.instructionalfair.co.uk
Duke Street, Wisbech, Cambs PE13 2AE

Routledge Falmer
www.routledgefalmer.com
11 New Fetter Lane, London EC4P 4EE

SEN Marketing
www.sen.uk.com
618 Leeds Road, Outwood, Wakefield, West Yorkshire
WF1 2LT

THRASS
www.thrass.co.uk

Whurr Publishers
www.whurr.co.uk

ICT suppliers

Crick Software
www.cricksoft.co.uk

Inclusive Technology
www.inclusive.co.uk

SEMERC
www.blackcatsoftware.com

Xavier Educational Software
www.xavier.bangor.ac.uk

Conclusion

This part of Chapter 6 has provided a sample of some of the resources and information websites that can help teachers and parents find out more on dyslexia. Dyslexia is a changing field with many new developments. It is important, therefore, that teachers acquire a basic understanding of dyslexia (which is the aim of this book) and are provided with the opportunity to keep up to date with developments in the field (the aim of this part of Chapter 6).

This book has provided teachers with an overview of dyslexia and has also provided them with the means to gain an understanding of dyslexia, therefore gaining more control over how they identify and deal with the barriers confronting children with dyslexia in the classroom. It is important that the effects of these barriers are minimized. One of the principal aims of this book is to reinforce the view that dyslexia need not be disabling. Accurate assessment, informed teaching and enlightened curriculum planning can all contribute to a successful educational outcome for all children with dyslexia.

References

Adams, M.J. (1990) *Beginning to Read: The New Phonics in Context*. Oxford: Heinemann.

Cowling, H. and Cowling, K. (1998) *Toe by Toe, Multisensory Manual for Teachers and Parents*. Bradford, UK: Toe by Toe.

Cowling, K. (2001) *Stride Ahead – An Aid to Comprehension*. West Yorkshire: Keda Publications.

Crowne, E. (2000) 'Inclusive Education: Access for all – Rhetoric or Reality', Offprints Booklet, pp. 119–31, *E 831 Professional Development for Special Educational Needs Co-Ordinators*. Milton Keynes: Open University Press.

Fawcett, A.J. and Nicolson, R.I. (1996) *The Dyslexia Early Screening Test*. London: The Psychological Corporation.

Gorrie, B. and Parkinson, E. (1995) *Phonological Awareness Procedure*. Northumberland: Stass Publications.

Hatcher, J. and Snowling, M.J. (2002) 'The Phonological Representations Hypothesis of Dyslexia: From Theory to Practice', in G. Reid and J. Wearmouth (eds) *Dyslexia and Literacy, Theory and Practice*. Chichester: John Wiley and Sons.

Johnson, M., Philips, S. and Peer, L. (1999) *Multisensory*

Teaching System for Reading (MTSR). Didsbury, UK: Special Educational Needs Centre, Didsbury School of Education, Manchester Metropolitan University.

Johnson, M. (2004) 'Dyslexia Friendly Schools – Policy and Practice', in G. Reid and A. Fawcett *Dyslexia in Context: Research, Policy and Practice*. London: Whurr Publications.

Keefe, J.W. (1987) *Learning Style – Theory and Practice*. Reston, VA: National Association of Secondary School Principals.

Lloyd, S.R. and Berthelot, C. (1992) *Self Empowerment: How to get what you want from life*. London: Kogan Page.

Medwell, J. (1995) 'A school policy for reading', in C. Gairns and D. Wray (eds) *Reading Issues and Direction*. Tamworth, England: NASEN (National Association of Special Education Needs).

Mosley, J. (1996) *Quality Circle Time in the Primary Classroom*. Cambridge: LDA.

Open University (2002) *Course materials E 801*. Milton Keynes: Open University Press.

Reid, G. (2003) *Dyslexia: A Practitioners Handbook* (3rd edn). Chichester: John Wiley and Sons.

Reid, G. and Kirk, J. (2001) *Dyslexia in Adults: Education and Employment*. Chichester: John Wiley and Sons.

Russell, S. (1993) *Phonic Code Cracker* (revised edn 2000). Glasgow: Jordanhill Publications.

Singleton, C. H. (1996) *COPS 1 Cognitive Profiling System*. Nottingham, UK: Chameleon Educational Ltd.

Thomson, M. and Chinn, S. (2001) 'Good Practice in the Secondary School', in A. Fawcett (ed.) *Dyslexia:*

Theory and Good Practice. London: Whurr Publications.

Tod, J. (2002) 'Individual Education Plans and Dyslexia: Some Principles', in G. Reid and J. Wearmouth (eds) *Dyslexia and Literacy, Theory and Practice*. Chichester: John Wiley and Sons.

Weedon, C. and Reid, G. (2001) *Listening and Literacy Index – A Group Test to Identify Specific Learning Difficulties*. London: Hodder and Stoughton.

Weedon, C. and Reid, G. (2003) *Special Needs Assessment Profile*. London: Hodder and Stoughton.